STEVEN BERKOFF

Plays Three

Ritual in Blood

Messiah

Oedipus

Introduced by
the author

faber and faber

First published in 2000
by Faber and Faber Limited
3 Queen Square, London WC1N 3AU
Published in the United States by Faber and Faber Inc.
an affiliate of Farrar, Straus and Giroux, New York

Typeset by Country Setting, Kingsdown, Kent CT14 8ES
Printed in England by Mackays of Chatham plc, Chatham, Kent

A CIP record for this book is available from the British Library

ISBN 0-571-20587-9

2 4 6 8 10 9 7 5 3 1

Contents

RITUAL IN BLOOD

THE JEWS OF ENGLAND (1290)

An Edward's England spat us out – a band
Foredoomed to redden Vistula or Rhine,
And leaf-like toss with every wind malign.
All mocked the faith they could not understand . . .

Israel Zangwill, 1902

Then said they unto him, Tell us we pray thee . . .
What is thine occupation? and whence comest thou?
what is thy country? and of what people art thou?
And he said unto them, I am an Hebrew; and I fear
the Lord, the God of heaven, which hath made
the sea and the dry land.

Jonah 1, 8–9

Introduction

HUGH OF LINCOLN
THE BLOOD RITUAL CHARGE

Ritual murder is one of the most monstrous charges that has ever been levelled against the Jewish race. Apparently the first recorded charge took place in England, in Norwich, in 1144. From thence it spread to France and Germany. The basis of the charge is that the Jews sought to murder and disembowel a Christian child in mockery of the crucifixion and then use its blood in secret ceremonies or for the Passover wafers. Although there is nothing in contemporary Jewish law, mythology or mysticism or folklore that requires human or animal blood, this did not deter any opportunist from pointing the finger at the Jews and inspiring a real blood bath. So in one sense the paradox is that the reverse was true. It was their detractors who sought blood, and plenty of it! Jews were frequently 'bled' dry for their money and taxed intolerably, but not too much to prevent them from earning more and becoming a convenient 'cash cow' to be milked whenever a crime could be pinned on them. Under the laws of the country the Jews were the King's property and thus crimes committed by them would draw huge fines in favour of the King. Consequently it became very convenient if you were in the Jews' debt – as many of the Barons were – to invent one. This would of course facilitate the arrest of the Jew and the dissolving of the debt.

Whilst performing as an actor in Lincoln, I happened to be walking through the impressive Lincoln Cathedral when I saw a plaque to Saint Hugh of Lincoln. Little Hugh was canonised many centuries ago and was the subject of a ritual murder charge. The inscription records

the supposed crucifixion of the eight-year-old boy but
adds that this legend brings no honour to Christianity.
However, I was struck by the extraordinary tale and it
stayed in my mind for many years until I decided to
research as much as I could on the subject itself in the
Reading Room of the British Museum. Though there
were no 'rolls' relating to this trial in particular, I found
much fascinating information regarding other trials and
debates where Jews were forced very often to defend
themselves in the public forum.

The blood libel, like a noxious virus, has erupted from
time to time throughout the world. The last case in a
civilised society was the accusation and arrest of Mendel
Beilis in Kiev, Russia, in 1911. This time however we
had something called the international press, and world
opinion was united against the trumped-up charges and
the authorities were obliged to release him. Sadly, in the
Middle Ages the depredations and villainies of anti-
Semitism were not so easily monitored. In researching
this play what struck me most forcibly was the incredible
extent to which the poison of anti-Semitism was part
of the fabric of the early church and how much the
more reactionary elements irrigated the earth for these
poisonous shoots to thrive. Curiously, Shakespeare's
Shylock is an offshoot of the blood charge, since Shylock
himself wields the knife, is bloodthirsty enough to use
it and is impervious to the cry for mercy from Portia.
What makes that play both fascinating and yet morally
untenable is Shylock's defence of his act as if speaking
for his race. The truth of the matter is that since the Jews
were forcibly expelled from England in 1290, their
property confiscated and their blood shed, there were
few, if any, Jews left. It was only in 1655 that Oliver
Cromwell, Lord Chief Protector, readmitted them,
recognising their importance in the Spanish and
Portuguese trade routes.

Characters

Rabbi Ben Barachyal
Copin
Jacob
Isaac
Naomi
Rabbi Ben Moses
Congregation
Luke
Beatrice
Edmund
Tilly
Idiot
Langley
Sheriff John
King
Father Arnold
Blind Man
First Priest
Second Priest
Monk
First Expert
Second Expert
Third Expert
First Financier
Second Financier
Archbishop
Judge
First Prosecutor
Second Prosecutor

Ritual in Blood was first performed by Nottingham Playhouse Company in Summer 2001.

Act One

SCENE ONE

*Two small boys are seen clambering over a garden wall –
it is a hot August day – the air is thick with garden
sounds and warm sunshine. They are both happily
engaged in poaching the apples that hang so temptingly
within arms' reach. The boys are brothers – the younger
one, Hugh, is eight and is being held by his older brother
Edmund, who is about eleven, to enable him to pick the
apples with both hands. Suddenly Edmund's grip relaxes
for a fatal moment causing his younger brother, who is
unable to cling to anything, to tumble over the wall.
Edmund peers over the wall and perceives by the
crumpled and twisted shape of Hugh that he is very
much dead. He has fallen into a shallow well sunk just
inside the garden wall – it is about seven feet deep and
practically dried up. Edmund is terror-stricken, scales
down the wall and runs home. The year is 1255, the
town is Lincoln, Henry III is on the throne.*

SCENE TWO

*From the well where Hugh lies dead, across the garden
and into the house of Copin, the Jewish money lender.
Several Lincoln Jews are in a conference concerning the
preparations for a wedding. Rabbi Ben Barachyal's
daughter is to marry Copin's son. They all wear a yellow
sign on their clothes.*

Copin To pray and not make noise – how is that
possible?

7

Isaac Whisper, how else?

Copin In two days our children must be married like criminals – like a shameful thing is taking place.

Rabbi Ben Barachyal Whose shame, Copin – theirs or ours? God will hear your whispers as well as your shouts, he's not deaf.

Jacob (*son of Copin*) Rabbi, why has the clergy prevailed upon the King to forbid us speaking our prayers aloud in our synagogue?

Isaac (*interjecting before Rabbi Ben Barachyal can answer*) Why does a nettle sting? It stings! You don't question it!

Rabbi Ben Barachyal Perhaps, my son, the priests have been waiting so long for a word from God, they think if they keep us quiet long enough, they might be able to hear it.

   Laughter.

So that is the least we can do to help.

Copin And for the King's protection for which we have been bled the sum of four hundred and twenty-two thousand pounds over the last seven years – that means nothing?

Isaac He's a heavy spender.

Copin How can he spend such a sum in seven years – he can't eat it?

Isaac His French Queen has expensive tastes – only the other day he gave her Cambridge – to soothe a quarrel – and then he is forced to finance the occasional adventure to the Holy Land to rout the 'perfidious' Saracen!

Copin (*sardonic*) Oh well! I suppose we must be grateful, Isaac – the King thinks so much of Israel that he's getting it ready for our return.

Rabbi Ben Barachyal That will not be long Copin – remember Isaiah's prophecy – 'The redeemed of the Lord shall return and come with singing in to Zion.'

Copin On that day Rabbi I would come . . . whispering!

SCENE THREE

By this time Edmund has just reached home, having run all the way from Copin's garden. His father Luke is eating – he has a not over-productive smallholding. Two other small children sit around the table. His mother Beatrice although in her mid-twenties has a middle-aged pallor through constant childbearing. Her whole being is permeated with a sense of resignation and she will grasp at anything, any gossip, any neighbour's suffering that temporarily alleviates her own.

Beatrice (*to Edmund as he goes to sit*) You wash before you sit down to your dinner – you look as if you've been dragged through a field of cow dung.

Luke Where's little-un – he'll get nought to eat knowing you – go fetch him Ed.

Edmund (*appearing unconcerned*) I don't know – he'll be along soon.

Beatrice Where's he gone then – you're supposed to look after him.

Edmund I did – but I lost him.

Luke What do you mean, lost him?

Edmund Hugh ran off when a man chased us – that's when I lost him.

Beatrice What? You been stealing again?

Edmund No honest – we were just climbing a wall and some man chased us – I went one way and Hugh another.

Luke You don't climb walls for nought – what were you stealing?

Edmund Only apples – they were hanging over the wall – he wouldn't have missed a few.

   Beatrice cuffs him.

Beatrice What! You want people to think we don't feed you?

Luke Oh leave him, Beatrice – who hasn't stolen apples – go on Ed – go find your brother and then you can eat.

Edmund (*hesitates*) Oh . . . he'll be all right – he can find his way can't he?

Luke Whose apples were you stealing?

Edmund From the big stone house on the hill.

Beatrice That's the Jew's house.

Luke (*suddenly interested*) And he's the one who chased you?

Edmund Yes, he came out after us – he had a big black beard and a big hat on – he couldn't run fast – but he ran after Hugh.

Beatrice (*cuffs him again*) I warned you never to go near that house – you know what they do – they're sorcerers – they eat up little boys them Jews do . . . they got horns haven't they Luke?

Luke I don't know.

Beatrice Well you're always borrowing money from him – haven't you peeked?

Luke He always keeps his hat on when I see him.

Beatrice He has to – that's to hide his horns. (*Shakes Edmund.*) Oh you make me cross – now you get out and find your brother before you get one crumb.

Edmund leaves house.

Luke If he's touched a hair on his head I'll kill him.

Beatrice He wouldn't dare.

Luke Is that true – that they sometimes eat little boys?

Beatrice Yes, I heard it somewhere that they take little babies and eat them up at Easter time.

Luke They couldn't be that evil surely?

Beatrice Ain't they? You'd be surprised what they get up to – why do you suppose the church only lets *them* be money lenders which our Good Lord forbade 'cause it's evil and therefore they'd be good at it . . . Do you still owe him much?

Luke Nearly twenty pounds.

Beatrice (*weary*) Oh God, Luke, we'll never pay that off.

Luke (*defensive*) What about Jack Langley – he's mortgaged so much, his land will be sold if he can't pay it!

Beatrice They'd take a man's own land off him!

Luke More than that – there's many an abbey that's lost its land through mortgage to them!

Beatrice That's really evil – something should be done about people like that.

Luke looks at her, not really comprehending her hatred but accepting it.

SCENE FOUR

A heavy knocking at the door of Copin's house. Three or four men including Luke stand at the door. Copin opens it – he is agitated, it is the morning of the wedding. A low murmuring ensues.

Copin Two days?

Luke Aye – two – that's the last time he was seen – breathing.

Copin I never saw your children two days ago.

Luke Edmund said he saw you – in fact you chased them.

Copin (*astonished*) I chased him!?

Luke For stealing apples.

Copin If he wanted apples he need only have asked.

Tilly (*one of the men*) Very Christian of you!

They chuckle.

Luke Ed, come here!

Edmund nervously appears from behind his father.

Were you chased by this man two days ago?

Edmund (*too embarrassed to look at him*) I er . . .

Luke Well, were you or weren't you – find your tongue lad.

Edmund nods mutely.

Copin I swear I never saw any of your children two days ago . . . Which children, I don't even know what they look like!

Luke (*struggling, less certain*) Mind you, it's no crime to chase away poachers stealing your fruit . . . I mean just *chasing* them's no crime – I do that.

Tilly (*backing Luke's uncertainty*) You wouldn't even do that Luke – you'd begrudge no one an apple – specially a mite!

Copin (*raising voice*) I never saw – I never chased – now please leave – my son's marriage is today – forgive me, but there is much to do.

Luke (*uncomfortably*) Ed – you sure you were chased by him?

Edmund, painfully embarrassed, hides behind father.

Tilly Of course he was – look at the boy, he's terrified – look at his face Luke!

Luke (*pushes Edmund in front of him – very unsure of himself now*) Now you speak what happened.

Edmund is unable to speak in front of Copin. Luke is hot with embarrassment – he twists Edmund's arm.

Go on, nobody's going to hurt you!

Edmund (*blurts out in pain*) He chased us over the wall – he chased us over the wall!!

Copin (*mortified*) How do you mean my son – that I leapt over that high wall after you like an eagle – did I throw my stick down and sprout wings – come, why are you saying these untrue things? (*Puts hands on Edmund's shoulders.*)

Luke (*remembering Beatrice's rumour, snatches Edmund from him and pushes Copin violently against door*) Don't touch him!

The other men are stirred to action by this outburst and move in menacingly. Copin's wife and son come to the door.

Naomi (*a shriek that alarms them for a moment*) Get away from here! Leave us in peace! Leave us! My husband harmed no one in his life – get out of here!

Jacob (*simply*) Why do you think my father would harm your child?

Tilly (*answering for Luke*) He was last seen here – that's why – we've heard things!

Jacob Things?

Luke (*awkwardly*) I mean – chasing's no crime – you don't want no one stealing your fruit – it's just that we haven't seen him – not since then.

Jacob Have you searched the woods – he may have injured himself climbing or fallen into a wolf trap.

Tilly Wolf trap eh! (*Snorts – makes gesture with hands elongating his nose to resemble a wolf, or Jew.*)

Jacob You're quite welcome to search the grounds and the woods behind the house if you wish – I would help you but I am to be married today.

Tilly (*smiling*) That's all right Master Jacob, we'll find our way around – I'm sure we don't want to disturb your wedding day.

The men go off.
Jacob closes the door – they stand around not knowing what to say to each other.

Copin (*numbly*) It's come!

Jacob (*knowing what he means*) What's come Father?

Copin *It's* come! The filthy blood lie! Like the plague it's come – a curse on their houses! Those sons of Ham, a curse on them!

Naomi (*restraining him*) Ben quiet! No one's accused.

Copin Then what were they doing? Bringing me gifts – blessing our wedding? Accused? No, they have condemned! Can you believe it! We kill children for Passover! We drink their blood! This is what these swine are taught.

Jacob No one believes that any more, Father.

Naomi No – not in Lincoln anyway – they have respect for us here – he'll probably find his boy – Luke's not a bad man – you'll see.

Copin So thank God it's not Passover. (*to Jacob*) Get ready for your wedding son – it's not right to keep your wife waiting on your wedding day – say nothing of this to anyone – we already have to whisper the service – let's not make it a dirge.

They laugh nervously – anxious to find some relief.

SCENE FIVE

Luke and his friends are seen beating the brush and undergrowth looking for Hugh's body – they have been joined by more people. They are searching round the area of Copin's house.

SCENE SIX

The wedding service. The daughter of the great scholar Rabbi Ben Barachyal is being married, consequently the heads of most of the leading Jewish families in England are there to do him honour. The service is solemn, conducted as stated in whispers. The Rabbi takes the scrolls out of the ark and kisses them. The service is conducted in Hebrew.

SCENE SEVEN

Two of the search party have entered the garden. One grimaces as he noses out something – holds his nose and grins supposing the smell to be from the latrines – curious, though, he goes to the source of the smell, which leads him to the well. The smell is Hugh's body decomposing under the hot summer sun. He shouts. People start climbing over the wall – the other man holds his legs while he lowers himself inside the well. As the man pulls him up, he pulls Hugh up by his ankles like a dead shark.

SCENE EIGHT

At the synagogue they are coming to the end of the service. The groom smashes the glass according to custom. Suddenly the door is thrust open – Luke stands there, his eyes glazed with hatred. In his arms he holds Hugh wrapped in a cloth. The service dwindles to an end – an awful silence ensues.

Rabbi Ben Moses (*who conducts the service*) You profane the house of God. Who are you? What do you want?

Luke (*takes cloth off body revealing Hugh's face*) The man . . . the man . . . who did this to my son.

Tilly His son's killer, that's what he wants.

> *Congregation shocked, murmuring and whispering.*
> *Luke points out Copin. Naomi lets out an ear-piercing*
> *scream and collapses.*

Rabbi Ben Moses (*goes to Luke*) Leave our temple – you stain the air with this vileness.

Luke With him we'll leave – Copin the Moneylender.

Copin (*terrified, hides behind the congregation*) They are mad – they have caught the sickness – the blood ritual!

> *Congregation murmuring in Yiddish and English –*
> *odd words emerge.*

Congregation Blood ritual! Oi vey! Vey is mere! (*etc.*)

> *The village idiot wanders into the synagogue*
> *fascinated by what is going on – sees one of the*
> *Rabbis hurriedly putting the sacred scrolls away.*

Idiot (*giggling*) What's he got there?

Tilly They've got their magic spells written on there – witchcraft and Jew magic.

> *The atmosphere is totally unreal. The congregation*
> *have been frozen up to now with fright, with Copin*
> *still hiding in the background.*

Langley (*friend of Luke's*) Let's get it then – that's evidence.

He attempts to snatch the scroll from the Rabbi, who holds on tightly to it.

Idiot (*jumping up and down*) Watch out! He'll turn you into a frog – he'll turn you into a frog! (*Squeals with delight.*)

Rabbi Ben Moses (*shouting*) I beg of you as you respect the sanctity of your own church to respect ours – let the Sheriff come and make some formal charge.

Bedlam breaks out as they search for Copin.

Copin (*screaming*) Our house is infested with vipers and serpents! A plague on them – get them off me!

Langley has succeeded in tearing the scrolls in half. He holds his half triumphantly in the air – women are screaming – two men attempting to interfere are struck with clubs – the idiot jumps around shouting with glee: 'Vipers and serpents – vipers and serpents!' Two or three men are dragging Copin out by his feet.

Luke (*speaks to crowd*) He's all we want – my son was found in his well – dead and done for – *we'll* take him to the Sheriff.

They drag him out.

Langley (*as he exits, holds up torn scroll*) We'll decipher your magic curses too – we'll find out your dirty witchcraft – one of our priests knows the tongue. (*Exits.*)

A general lamenting ensues. Various men praying, saying the Kaddish – prayer for the dead. Copin's wife, weeping, being attended to by a woman. Jacob comforts his new wife Judith – he is dazed, having been hit by one of the clubs. Suddenly he springs to life as if revolted by the lamentable sight.

Jacob What! Dogs are we? Whimpering? Prayers for the dead! No more cowing. Did you hear me! Let there be no more cowing!

Rabbi tries to restrain Jacob's rising hysteria. Jacob goes to door as if to follow the mob, and seeking support.

Are we dogs? Are we? Or men!

They all look uncertain – whether to go with him or to stay. A man steps forward.

Man Men Jacob, so God help me!

Jacob Chaim! Good, Chaim the butcher! Bring your knives Chaim – your slaughterer's knives – we'll give them a ritual murder!

Various men come forward one at a time, tentatively – some more positive.

Various Men Not cowards Jacob!
We are together!
We'll come Jacob!
The filth – the evil filth!

Several men are going to the door to follow Jacob when, above the tumult and shouting, a sudden curdling wail of the Shofar, the ram's horn, is heard which the Rabbi Ben Moses has used to control them. At the sound of this they are caught frozen, silenced by this old instrument of alarm.

Rabbi Ben Moses Children, search your judgements! What, are you mad? Need you the ram's horn to make you think? Like sheep you go to the sacrifice!

Jacob Rabbi – the ram's horn was an alarm for King David's army when the enemy approached . . . to strike!

Rabbi Ben Moses (*seeking a rational answer to suffering*) Are we an army? Are we? Then where is King David?

Congregation look at each other uncertain what to do.

Every year on the Day of Atonement the scrolls of fate open before the Lord – in these scrolls every man's hand has written his deeds of the year passed – God reads the entries and pronounces judgement – only *he* fixes our destinies – decides who shall fall and who shall rise – only *he* decides who shall live in peace and who shall stumble in misery – Jacob do you hear me!

Isaac *And* the Archbishop of Canterbury, may his soul rot in hell! But this is not the Day of Atonement, Rabbi! Is it the will of God that our beloved cousins in York should perish by their own hand – is it God's will that they should be destroyed in Nuremburg! – did the Day of Judgement come for them to be burned alive in London, inspired by the villainous Thomas à Becket . . . was that God's will? – No! God helps his fighters not his martyrs.

Voice Not like sheep we go to the sacrifice Rabbi – like Jews!

General uproar.

Rabbi Ben Barachyal Children – let us not be divided – a terrible mistake has happened here today and we shall rectify it – the evil blood crime can no longer be imputed to us. Do we not have a charter from the King protecting us against the mob and should we not use it in a civil way? I and other representatives shall appeal to the Sheriff on Copin's behalf. Be not heavy-hearted, this is Lincoln . . . it cannot happen here . . .

SCENE NINE

The Sheriff, John of Lexington, who has a notable reputation as a Jew-baiter, is questioning Copin in one of the chambers of the court. His secretary sits with him. Copin and Rabbi Ben Barachyal are seated on the other side with Copin's son. The secretary is taking notes.

Sheriff John (*coldly surveying Copin, but relaxed – he feels he has trapped his quarry – he wishes to enjoy it*) In a well – head first with his skull crushed in – aah – poor little boy – poor little mite . . . Why should you wish to harm an innocent child?

Copin Why indeed – for stealing apples? I am no barbarian.

Sheriff John You're a moneylender. (*Smiles at his equation.*)

Copin That's right – I make money grow – that's my trade – there is no profit in cadavers.

Sheriff John Really Jew – I would have thought you'd make a profit in anything.

Copin Not really Sheriff – since your laws forbid us to trade in little else but money, I'll leave the cadavers to you.

Sheriff John (*eating his rage*) Careful Jew – your disrespect for the dead will hang you!

Copin That is if your disrespect for the living has not hung me first.

Sheriff John (*eyeing him coldly, hating everything about him*) What's your implication Jew?

Jacob (*calmer now, attempts to negotiate the situation*) Forgive my father's speech – he has suffered much today – he would harm no one – recall how many years we have lived peaceably in Lincoln – my father has rendered the community no small service.

Sheriff John We are not malicious men, although I am aware of how your people are prejudiced against us – but facts speak loudest – today a small child is found in *your* well – the last time he was seen, your father was chasing him with a stick.

Copin Lies – chase?! My legs are crippled from the ague!

Jacob It is true what my father says – he could never have climbed the wall as the child claims – furthermore there are witnesses including the learned Rabbi here and myself who were with him that morning – we were all with him during the time stated.

Sheriff John How interesting that your father should have *so* many witnesses at the appropriate time – and how often have these same learned men been together?

Jacob To my knowledge only once.

Sheriff John (*quickly*) Only once – what a coincidence!

Jacob My wedding – it was to discuss that . . .

Sheriff John Which happened to be just at the time little Hugh was picking apples . . . or was it to conspire together – for is it not well known that at certain times of the year the Jews collect together to arrange their heinous crimes – namely the killing of a Christian child.

Copin No! Never! Filthy lies!

Sheriff John (*continuing*) . . . And is it not stated in your magic Talmud that your race cannot be saved to return to the Holy Land unless a Christian child is sacrificed every year?

Copin Treachery!

Sheriff John And was that not in fact the purpose of
your meeting two days ago when suddenly an
opportunity presented itself to you in the shape of that
innocent child . . . there you all were, planning your
infamous crime, when little Hugh appeared in your
garden like the Devil's omen – how could you resist it!

Copin A plague on the spreader of such filth – never
have we been guilty of this.

Sheriff John As you say every time you are condemned
for it.

Jacob (*trying to keep control*) Sheriff John, today I was
married to this man's daughter Judith – she is my wife –
it was to discuss this wedding that brought these men
together, not murder – a wedding, my wedding – can't
you understand that – what must we do to convince you!

Sheriff John (*ignoring him*) Little Hugh's broken body
was found in Copin's well . . .

Rabbi Ben Barachyal Sir, it grieves me to find that
Christians still believe that the laws of the Jews sanction
this appalling story, while the very reverse is true. Why
ascribe every accident, every murder even, wherever it
chance to occur, to the Jews? Did not his Holiness Pope
Innocent IV officially contradict the baseless and fiendish
imputations in his Bull in 1247 which our good King has
taken pains to support?

Sheriff John The King's protection renders no one
immune from common law.

Rabbi Ben Barachyal Nor would we demand immunity
from these crimes – but first let these crimes be proven!
This gentleman could no longer leap walls nor chase
sprightly children than I fly to the moon.

Sheriff John (*looks at Rabbi with a smirk as if to say, perhaps you can*) It is not within my jurisdiction to examine you further . . . that will be done by experts.

Rabbi Ben Barachyal We shrink from no enquiry within the law.

Sheriff John Good!

They all wait, watching each other – Sheriff takes notes from secretary and starts to read them.

You may go . . .

Copin (*astonished*) Go? I'm free?

Sheriff John For the time being – but don't let your sheep wander far, Rabbi.

As they exit he calls after them.

Incidentally Copin, I believe Hugh's father is heavily mortgaged to you?

Copin He is mortgaged for twenty pounds.

Sheriff John And he is finding it difficult to repay, in view of his large family?

Copin I have not pressed him.

Sheriff John (*annoyed, having expected a different answer*) In consideration of his grief it would not go badly with you if you relieved his difficulties . . .

Copin Did I cause his grief?

Sheriff John (*abruptly*) Stony heart! Think well on it Jew – a little magnanimity is sometimes good for you . . .

Copin (*trying to read Sheriff's mind – is it money he wants? After a pause*) Ah! But would it be?

Sheriff John (*toying with him*) Is not kindness its own reward?

Copin Turning the other cheek is not in our book!

Sheriff John (*threatening*) Do not bargain with *me*, Jew!

Copin (*looks to Jacob and Rabbi for an indication – they cannot help him – Copin knows there is no quarter – simply*) I shall be happy to relieve his difficulties and lighten their sorrows for the loss of a son.

They bow and exit.

Sheriff John Arnold!

A thin-faced priest comes out from behind a screen where he has been listening – he is pale and sweaty and suffers slightly from a nervous twitch which occasionally disrupts his long passive face.

Arnold (*they stare at each other for some moments as if to decide what to do or say – Arnold weighs words like gold*) Hmmn . . .

Sheriff John Well? . . .

Arnold (*cunning*) Cunning! Oh they're cunning, yes, but not careful – not by half.

Sheriff John Meaning?

Arnold The bribe to his accuser has tied him to the stake . . .

Sheriff John Aah!

Arnold But not quite lit the faggots.

Sheriff John Oh! . . .

Arnold Step at a time!

Sheriff John Indeed yes.

Arnold But we need more evidence – the old Jew chasing the boy – that's not good – somebody else must have done the chasing.

Sheriff John (*thoughtful*) Hmmn! . . .

Arnold But I'm convinced – certainly I'm convinced, but more witnesses are needed – and evidence of the style of killing.

Sheriff John But there is only the boy's brother and as you heard, his evidence is weak.

Arnold (*thoughtful*) Yes . . . a similar problem was solved in Blois – the Jews crucified a Christian child because they needed the blood for Passover cakes, but there was only one witness – being a fair tribunal they were reluctant to condemn on the evidence of just one witness – so the water test was applied – the witness was conveyed to the river in a boat filled with water – the witness did not sink, thus proving the truth of his testimony.

Sheriff John What became of the Jews?

Arnold Count Theobald issued an order condemning the entire Jewish population to death by fire – some could have saved their lives if they had acknowledged Christianity – you see how fair it was – but they were like men possessed and refused the noble offer.

Sheriff John The water test?

Arnold Yes – it was most popular then but I don't think the Earl of Cornwall acknowledges that matter.

Sheriff John So? . . .

Arnold I must see the body to ascertain the method of killing – the wounds will speak louder than anything – the ritual cuts are unmistakable – poor child!

Sheriff John (*gleeful*) Good Arnold, good – do everything that you can – we'll have our fires in Lincoln yet!

Arnold (*disdainful*) I shall do all I can – for God's sake, Sheriff John, not for yours.

Sheriff John (*icily*) Yes of course! Of course!

Arnold (*after a short silence*) He must be very wealthy, think you?

Sheriff John In the extreme.

Arnold Hmmn . . . our local church is badly in need, Sheriff John – for a new window – also we have commissioned thirty misericords with most ornate carving.

Sheriff John Isn't that an extravagance?

Arnold Our aged clergy must have somewhere to sit, Sheriff John, besides Winchester and Gloucester have sixty each – even Exeter has fifty . . . (*Waits in vain for some kind of offer, which is not forthcoming.*)

Sheriff John How much money do you need?

Arnold (*becoming alert*) Oh . . . I think five hundred pounds would be satisfactory.

Sheriff John Then I am sure God will guide you to the source of it . . . (*Smiles an implication.*)

Arnold (*affecting not to notice it*) Confession under torture is permissible.

Sheriff John They don't always confess.

Arnold Aaah! I have heard from men whom I hold in the highest esteem that when torturing an unyielding body on the rack it is necessary to apply a burning wick to its shadow on the floor because the scheming devil may sometimes transpose the body where the shadow seems to lie!

27

Sheriff John (*very interested*) I see . . . that's why they appear so stubborn.

Arnold Of course Sheriff John, of course.

SCENE TEN

Home of Luke and Beatrice. Luke is drunk, having been celebrating the dissolving of his debts. In his stupor, he has turned on his son and is boxing him round the ears.

Edmund Oh no don't, please Dad, don't! – I didn't tell lies, I swear!

Luke Name me for a fool would you – climb the wall and chase Hugh! Why the old Jew can barely walk!

Edmund He did! He did!

Beatrice Oh leave him, Luke – the Sheriff believed you, didn't he, and the priests, so what the hell – besides they let you off all that money – they wouldn't have done that if they didn't believe you, would they?

Luke (*turning on her*) You stupid bitch! Suppose they found out something else – I mean they had another witness, I mean that could happen – couldn't it – they ain't locked the Jew up – he's free – so they ain't sure are they – then we're in trouble aren't we – giving false evidence and that . . . ay?

Beatrice They wouldn't do nothing, even so, not for a Jew . . . no they wouldn't do nothing, don't you fret.

Luke No? Your wit's sluggish woman! They're the Baron's servants – their bankers when they're short of coin!

Beatrice They believe you, so what you on about – we've got our money!

Luke Yes – but *I* want to know. (*He cuffs Edmund hard.*) You can tell when he's lying – he takes on that furtive look in his eyes, like a hunted rat! (*Cuffs again and twists Edmund's arm.*) I'll twist it off – just tell the truth son and I'll leave you be.

Edmund (*crying out in pain*) It weren't my fault Dad – it weren't my fault – he did it himself!

Luke What!?

Edmund You won't hit me no more if I tell you?

Luke I'll hit you some more if you don't.

Edmund He slipped – I tried to hold on but he was too far away – the branch didn't hold.

Luke (*sobering fast*) Slipped!

Beatrice (*quickly shocked*) Oh my God! Oh my God!

Edmund He fell in the well on the other side – it weren't my fault!

Luke He fell in – himself!

Beatrice Oh my God!

Edmund (*nods*) I tried to hold him – I swear I tried.

Beatrice Oh my good God!

Luke (*raging at Beatrice*) *Shut your mouth, woman*! . . . Why didn't you fish him out – why did you just leave him there . . . Why didn't you tell us?

Edmund I was scared – I called him but he didn't answer – his body was all twisted funny – I was scared, that's why I ran away.

Beatrice (*bursts into tears*) Poor little Hugh.

Luke You're talking the truth now aren't you?

Edmund Yes – I was scared – you'd beat me if I told you what happened.

Luke I'll beat you black and blue for lying, rather. (*Advances menacingly.*)

Beatrice Enough now Luke – he's had enough for now. (*Signals Edmund to get out of his father's drunken route.*) Go on – get out!

Edmund slinks out quickly.

Luke (*lurches forward sadistically*) Leave me – let me at him!

Their actions are stopped by a knocking at the door. Luke goes to door and opens it. The priest Arnold stands there in the murky evening gloom – framed in the doorway with the rain dripping off him, for a second he has the appearance of an apparition. Edmund whisks out as Arnold comes in. Beatrice hides wine flask. Luke thinks he has seen a ghost.

Oh! . . . it's you Father Arnold.

Luke stares awkwardly at him and Arnold walks past him, seeing that he is not being invited in.

You gave me a scare for a moment – what with the rain and thunder.

Arnold Seemed to have scared the little one, too.

Beatrice Oh! He's wild tonight.

Luke (*trying to be sociable and not drunk*) The gods are in bad humour tonight, eh! Ha! Ha!

Arnold (*quietly*) The who? . . .

Luke (*quicky*) Oh Lord! . . . A manner of speaking, you know – I didn't mean that I . . .

Arnold (*interrupting*) I came to see if I could be of comfort to you in your pain.

Beatrice Oh thank you Father – you've been so kind to us already.

Luke Yes indeed – we don't know what to say, especially about the money and that . . .

Arnold (*eyes concealed bottle*) I see you've been putting it to some use already!

Luke (*sheepishly looks at bottle*) It was just a drop you know . . .

Beatrice (*hot with shame, prostrates herself at Arnold's feet*) Oh forgive us Father – please – Luke and I – we were so sick with grief we wanted to ease the pain. (*Starts sobbing.*) Please understand.

Luke That's true Father – it's only something to stem the grief.

Arnold (*with oily compassion, adoring attention*) God likes your grief – he wants your tears pure – they're libations to him expressing your feelings for one of his children returned before its time.

Beatrice Oh Father – little Hugh – do you think he's happy there?

Arnold Very happy – he's an angel there – little children are turned into angels – that's what he is.

Beatrice (*beatific*) A little angel!

> *Arnold takes Beatrice by the hand and sits her down, remains holding her hand.*

Arnold I never saw him – was he a happy child? . . . or does it pain you to talk of him?

Luke (*eager to make some capital*) Not at all Father – not at all – he was a game little boy, approaching nine years, a bit adventurous, you know . . .

Beatrice But a lovely nature – that's what everyone loved about him – he'd be only too happy to help anyone . . .

Luke Oh he would too – he was about so high, (*indicates*) with a kind of greeny eyes, they were a strange colour.

Beatrice (*factually*) They were blue-green with little auburn freckles – with rusty colour hair – his hair was so beautiful, he still had his baby curls – so pretty . . .

Luke You'd think he was a girl sometimes, so pretty he was.

Beatrice (*defensively*) But strong – he was scared of no one – daring he was.

Luke (*reacting*) I didn't say he wasn't did I – of course he was strong – I *said* he was game, didn't I – it was his *hair*!

Beatrice It were lovely, his hair – soft and curly like a little bird's nest.

Luke (*becoming exasperated*) From a distance sometimes he looked like a girl, that's all I'm saying!

Arnold (*coming between them*) He sounds a veritable angel – I am sad never to have seen him.

Beatrice (*quietly*) If he'd been a little less daring he might be alive today.

Luke throws her a look to reveal nothing.

Arnold (*having accepted Copin's guilt*) Tragic – absolutely tragic – did you never warn him to keep away from the Jew houses?

Beatrice Oh did I warn him! More than once, too – didn't I Luke?

Luke Oh yes! She was always telling him that . . .

Beatrice But you know what little children are.

Arnold Too innocent to appreciate the dangers that befall them.

Luke (*searching, cautious*) They're sure the Jews did it – are they?

Arnold Of course we are – aren't you?

Luke Oh yes I am – I mean he was found in their well weren't he – only as they let him go I thought . . .

Arnold In his overwhelming care that there should be no shreds of doubt, Sheriff John released the Jew in order that he may be examined properly – he is a compassionate man is Sheriff John.

Luke I can't understand why anyone would do such a thing.

Arnold Of course you can't – you do not converse with devils – how could you know their ways . . . May I see him?

Luke See him?

Arnold Yes – I should very much care to see him before he is finally laid to rest in the morning.

Luke He's there already.

Arnold (*shocked*) What!

Luke We had to – he'd been out in the sun for two days you see, Father, and . . . forgive me, but he was smelling a bit . . .

Arnold (*cold*) Who gave permission?

Luke The Bishop at the parish – he said it would be all right and he would perform the burial rites tomorrow.

Beatrice (*sensing something*) Have we done something wrong – have we been over-hasty?

Arnold (*down to business*) Did your son bear any unusual marks upon him?

Luke Marks?

Arnold Wounds, if you like?

Luke (*looks at Beatrice, tries to determine what Arnold expects*) What? Injuries from his fall you mean?

Arnold (*suddenly*) Fall?

Beatrice (*to Luke*) When he was *thrown* into the well. (*to Arnold*) Is that what you mean?

Arnold I wish to spare your agony but I must be open with you – every year the Jews choose a Christian child in a town in England and kill him to celebrate our Lord's crucifixion.

Luke The devils!

Arnold Exactly – the town is chosen by lots and certain Jews are delegated to carry it out – this time it is Lincoln – you've not heard of this?

Beatrice I heard something about them killing little children . . .

Arnold The child is martyred in the same way they martyred our Lord – they pierce his body and drink his warm blood . . .

Beatrice (*feeling faint*) Oh no!

Arnold (*carrying on, savouring the story*) Often they open the martyr's body and disembowel him –

Luke What's that Father?

Arnold Using his entrails for magic purposes – the blood they use for making cakes. All over England year after year, this gruesome ceremony is enacted. In their desperate search for blood they have been known to steal the Eucharist, the precious wafer, and stab it to bleed Christ.

Luke (*amazed*) For God's sake, the wafer itself bleeds? It can do that?

Arnold It is so. As Our Lord's body enters the wafer, it has been seen to bleed when abused . . .

Luke (*incredulous*) Even when it's made from flour after all, from the wheat in the fields? . . .

Arnold (*smiling benevolently*) When you take Communion what do you think we mean when we say the blood and flesh of Jesus?

Luke In his memory like . . . not real – but pretending . . .

Arnold You mean symbolically representing?

Luke Yes, that's what I meant – symbolic!

Arnold Know you this, that Our Lord is actually in the wine, actually in the wafer, that he has put part of his body there for us to make true his command that we should eat his flesh and drink his blood in celebration of his agony on the cross.

Luke But Father – I know it sounds stupid – but how does Our Lord's body eke out so far – I mean all those people – all of us eating . . . and drinking . . .

Arnold Because he is everywhere and can divide himself just as in the same way did he not divide the five loaves and the two fishes for the multitudes – for the five thousand.

Luke (*not really believing but accepting*) Oh just to see that now – so they stab the holy wafer, do they, and it really bleeds!

Arnold Of course, of course, that's the only way they can attack Our Lord's body when they do not stab and crucify infants instead. We must put a stop once and for all to their heinous crimes . . . (*intently*) Did you not notice these particular wounds on Hugh?

Luke (*uncertain what to say*) I didn't really look close – I was that upset, you see.

Beatrice kicks Luke's foot under table.

But I did see he was wounded.

Beatrice I did! He had those strange marks on his body – like regular marks – Ooh the fiends! . . . that what they did to him – animals!

Arnold (*exhilarated*) You should have spoken earlier – you have buried the evidence of their sorcery – never mind – I'll speak to the Bishop – we'll exhume his body tomorrow.

Beatrice Tomorrow?

Arnold Forgive me, but it must be done – their evil must be witnessed. (*inspired*) Your son, Beatrice Tanner, is our first martyr in Lincoln and shall be buried as a martyr – good night. (*He exits in an exalted mood.*)

They both stand transfixed for a moment and then Luke starts moaning.

Luke Oh no! No! No! What have you done, woman? (*Throws himself in chair.*) You mad? What are you?!

Beatrice What are you, husband? – didn't you hear him – they do this every year.

Luke Well they didn't do it to ours, did they, eh? . . .
And when they find out that he fell in himself, they
won't believe anything else we say! They'll hang me for
giving false witness – all because of that little rat. (*Starts
jumping round the room, goes beserk, looking for
Edmund.*) WHERE IS HE?!

Beatrice They won't find out! . . . Don't lose your senses!

Luke Won't find out? They're going to examine him in
the morning, you thick fool.

Beatrice (*hard*) That gives you all night . . .

Luke (*silence – unbelieving*) Have I married a dolt –
have I? . . .

Beatrice (*urgently*) Think husband, Copin's gold is lying
there waiting – maybe for us – sure, why not – we'd be
well looked after . . . they need the evidence – *give* it to
them!

Luke (*fearful*) Oh no! I can't do that! Not that! That's
devil's work!

Beatrice Little Hugh's dead now – he won't feel nothing
– anyway he said they do it every year, that's what he
said, didn't he? And who knows, this year it could be
Lincoln – like this, we prevent it happening again. Go on
– you know you can do it – you've got to!

Luke (*trying to imagine it*) Oh, that's terrible.

Beatrice You got no choice now.

Luke takes a huge draught of wine.

Luke That's not for me, that's not . . . opening graves
and . . . doing . . . (*Stifles a retch.*) Oh, I'm sick Beatrice.

Beatrice Listen, they dig him up in the morning and find
he's just fallen, eh? . . . Then what? . . . Come on – it's
dead flesh after all.

37

Luke (*weakly*) How? How do I do it Beatrice? . . .

Beatrice Just as he described it . . . there's no one at the churchyard now.

At this moment Edmund slinks in.

Luke Here Eddy . . . come here a moment.

Edmund runs behind his mother.

Edmund Don't hit me no more – don't let him hit me no more.

Luke I won't hit you – come here. (*Edmund does.*) Now you remember that story you said about the Jew chasing you both . . .

SCENE ELEVEN

The parish church the following morning. The rain has been falling all night, the atmosphere inside the church is damp and heavy – Hugh's torn body lies in ceremony covered by a cloth revealing only the face. The priest is coming to the end of his sermon before Hugh is finally buried. A large group are praying and marching including Luke and Beatrice and Edmund, who sports a black eye. The ceremony is performed according to traditional Catholic rites, the mass may be sung.

Arnold (*about to give communion*) Daily does Christ wash us from our sins in his own blood when remembrance of his blessed passion is rehearsed at the altar; when the creature of bread and wine, by the unspeakable hallowing of the spirit, is transferred into the sacrament of his flesh and blood.

People come forward. One person drops a couple of crumbs of the wafer.

Be careful! Let no particles fall, for what you lose would be to you as if you had lost some of your members – tell me, if anybody had given you gold dust would you not hold fast to it with all care lest some of it fall. Must you not then be even more careful with that which is more precious than gold and diamonds. Now sanctify yourself by receiving the blood of Christ . . . Oh Lord we have eaten the body crucified for us, and we have drunk the holy blood shed for us . . . (*his voice becoming edged with hysteria*) And may Christ's blood wash away the sins of our enemies who mock his crucifixion – whose wrath feeds on the innocent – who sacrifice the Pascal lamb in the shape of our little babies –

Loud murmuring from congregation.

– with a gnashing and grinding of teeth – but let Christ's compassion forgive them –

Murmurs of dissent

– for they know not what they do . . . Yes forgiveness! For they are sheep without a shepherd – wandering without purpose – ordained by God to be saved when they receive Our Lord.

Loud murmurings. A Blind Man comes from out of the congregation.

Blind Man (*with tears in his eyes*) Let me know him Father, for I cannot see his face.

The Priest guides the Blind Man's fingers over Hugh's face and then he wipes away his tears – suddenly he lets out a loud moan.

Aaaah! . . . God save me!

People gather round him murmuring 'What is it?' etc.

My eyes! . . . My eyes – I can see!

Second Priest (*to Arnold*) His hands were accidentally anointed with some moisture on the child's face and then as he wiped his eyes – he received a miracle!

Arnold Truly, Hugh is a martyr.

Crowd goes mad, weeping and shouting – odd words are shouted out: 'God strike them!' 'No, he gives us the power to do it for him!' . . . 'Destroy!' 'Kill!' etc, etc.

What you see now is the wonder of God working in his house – a sign! . . . to show his love to you – do not leave his house with hatred in your hearts – for you will have no room for his love – justice! Let us show the Jew that he will achieve justice – not his biblical vengeance!

Crowd Did they give that to little Hugh?!

A strong voice from the back of the crowd surprises them. A Franciscan monk has come to see the body.

Monk Did not Jesus also say, 'Let he who is innocent cast the first stone'? Why do you assume his guilt before he is tried?

Crowd are stunned for a moment and then turn on him, marching out of the church, pushing him aside. He picks himself up and after looking curiously at Arnold, who is surveying him contemptuously, follows them.

Arnold (*to Blind Man*) Come . . .

He leads him into an ante-room. Arnold transfers a small heavy bag which tinkles slightly as it is handed to 'Blind' Man.

'Blind' Man Thank you Father . . . if there is anything else I can do.

Arnold Vanish into the air – failing that – go to London
– spread the news of your 'miracle'.

'Blind' Man exits.
    Second Priest enters beaming radiantly.

Second Priest In all my years here Father, I have never
seen such a strong sign – praise be to God . . .

Arnold Our first martyr, Robert . . . our very first
martyr! . . .

SCENE TWELVE

*Copin's home has been ransacked. Inside sits his wife in
the centre of chaos. She has her husband's prayer shawl
around her, her head is completely shaved, it being the
custom of orthodox wives to use a wig. She is singing
over and over again the first line of the Kaddish.*

Naomi (*singing*) Yit – gaddal we-yit-kadash shemeh
rabba. (*etc.*)

*Jacob has never seen his mother's head bare. He finds
her wig and gives it to her. She does not look at him
but stares ahead unseeing and chanting. He then
places it on her head. She turns on him in an animal
rage throwing her wig across the room – with tears in
his eyes Jacob again approaches her with the wig –
her rage is less harmful to him than seeing her like
this.*

Jacob Please Mama – come on, please.

*He again tries to put wig on. She lets him this time.
He folds her in his arms.*

Oh God, save us – do not turn away from us now – hold

us unto you, are we not your chosen – then let us suffer no more – haven't we suffered enough as your chosen – you do not need our agony, so spare us all pain and protect your children – your innocent children who love you – yes, love you through the pain – are you listening to us God – can you hear me – yes, of course you can . . . (*Starts to weep.*) . . . or have you stopped listening . . . have you . . . or are you deaf! DEAF . . . OR DEAD!!

SCENE THIRTEEN

A dungeon in the local prison. Copin has been arrested and beaten. He is chained to a bench. No one has been allowed to see him except a preliminary group of experts who are questioning him in a semi-circle – four or five, including Arnold. Copin's face is bloody and swollen.

Arnold Last night the earth vomited up your crimes, which were too vile to be contained in it – the coffin containing the martyr Hugh, buried in all innocence by his father, was found this morning exposed – *on top of the earth*.

Copin (*weakly*) On top of the earth . . . in the earth . . . I know nothing.

First Expert It is as if the earth wished Hugh's body to be sanctified of the act of murder.

Second Expert Astonishing . . . and in a similar way Our Lord's body could not be contained in his tomb.

First Expert (*persuasively*) Why did you bleed the child?

Copin does not answer.

Is it because your Talmud instructs you to?

Silence.

Does it not say that 'The soul of all flesh is the blood thereof' . . . Therefore is not blood particularly sacred to your tribe?

Copin just stares at him, swollen and numb.

Come, admit – your own book says that.

Copin (*spits out*) It doesn't say 'shed blood'!

Second Expert Doesn't your God ask for blood on the sacrificial altar? – Blood! . . . as a means of atonement – Leviticus, Chapter 17 – what a demonic instruction – the demanding – the shedding of blood in a holy place!

Copin Animal blood!

Second Expert When human is not available!

First Expert (*to Second*) Please! (*mock admonition*) . . . You are not alone Copin, I know. You were selected by your Elders and had no choice but to enact their instructions, namely the crucifying of a child – how it must have weighed heavily on you . . . Of course you begged the Rabbi to release you from this task . . . but that would have brought your own punishment . . . perhaps even death . . . *WE UNDERSTAND* . . . Confess – who made you do it?

First Expert Nobody's here Copin – we are alone – nobody need ever know – come, tell us. (*Silence.*)

Third Expert What is the value of blood to you – to use in Passover biscuits? . . . to drink? (*Silence.*) Do you not bathe in human blood to cure disease? . . . Why did you cut out Hugh's heart? . . . Did you eat it? (*Silence.*) . . . or burn it on the altar? (*Silence.*)

Arnold Come Jew . . . save yourself – confess yourself to us and we will help you – confess your terrible secrets –

you will find immense relief. We know that you, as a God-fearing Jew, do not suddenly take upon yourself the role of murderer – your ailments prove that someone must have helped you.

Copin Let me see Rabbi Barachyal.

Arnold (*to experts*) That's his adviser. (*to Copin*) He won't help you Copin – confess yourself – free yourself – you hold your life in your hands.

Copin Rabbi Barachyal!

Arnold He cannot help you Copin – he mesmerises you – you are free of all influence to confess. Relieve yourself of the terrible weight. (*Silence.*)

Second Expert Ignorant Jew, do you not know that you are condemned already out of the mouth of one of your own kind? – a convert, Theobald of Cambridge . . .

Copin Apostate muck!

Sheriff John Careful Copin – the flames do not distinguish between the blasphemer and murderer.

Copin (*suddenly breaking*) THIS IS MY GOD AND I WILL PRAISE HIM – THE GOD OF MY FATHERS AND I WILL EXALT HIM!

Sheriff John Confession under torture, Copin, is less worthy of you than confession given freely.

Copin (*becoming crazed, speaks in Yiddish*) [Help me! Help me oh God!]

Sheriff John (*to guard*) Take him downstairs – just two turns of the rack – don't break him yet.

Copin (*rants on possessed*) Innocent! Innocent! Innocent!

First Expert (*over Copin's raves*) Surely it would be better if he were counselled by his Rabbi first.

Sheriff John What difference if he won't confess?

First Expert The difference of giving a prejudiced impression – that we denied him solace of his priest.

Sheriff John (*to guard*) Send for Rabbi Barachyal and let no one else in. (*to First Expert*) We certainly do not wish to appear prejudiced!

Rabbi Ben Barachyal enters – takes in situation at a glance, bows to them.

Rabbi Ben Barachyal May I be permitted to say immediately that nowhere in Judaic work, oral or textual, will you find recommendation of the crime this man is accused of.

First Expert (*gently*) Learned Rabbi, what is the sixth commandment?

Rabbi Ben Barachyal Thou shalt not murder, given to Moses on the holy tablets at Mount Sinai.

First Expert And the seventh commandment?

Rabbi Ben Barachyal Thou shalt not commit adultery.

First Expert Has no man killed? Has no man committed adultery, merely because they are not recommended?

The experts smile at each other. Having outwitted the famed Rabbi – they are about to leave.

Rabbi Ben Barachyal (*as they exit*) Many men are tempted to break commandments including the eighth – thou shalt not bear false witness against thy neighbour – the most sacred one.

First Expert (*turning at door, senses his implication*) Really Rabbi – you surprise me – I would have thought the commandment against murder (*staring at Copin*) could not be more sacred.

Rabbi Ben Barachyal If you would not bear false witness – then how could you murder – if you would not injure even a man's name – how could you injure his body? (*intently*) Therefore, 'Thou shalt not bear false witness' is the more sacred, because it is the most easily broken – it only needs the bad breath of venom . . . Release this man Sheriff John, he is innocent.

Sheriff John Unfortunately the evidence overwhelmingly blows in the other direction.

Rabbi Ben Barachyal Give me every shred of this 'evidence' that I may refute it!

Sheriff John In time – this is a preliminary examination and we are interrupting it to let you advise your colleague . . . Advise him well, Rabbi – a confession would stop here and prevent much suffering.

They exit.

Rabbi Ben Barachyal takes out a cloth and wipes Copin's swollen face.

Copin I am a dead man, Rabbi.

Rabbi Ben Barachyal Dead! You're full of life, Copin – there are no signs of death on you . . . they cannot kill you – this is what pains them – they will beat, they will purge, they will fine – but they cannot kill.

Copin Since when?

Rabbi Ben Barachyal (*trying to cheer him*) We are not their property – the King sold his rights in us for a huge sum to the Earl of Cornwall his brother – this is what annoys them. Under the King, they could kill with impunity – we then paid the King with blood money for protection – not so with the Earl of Cornwall, though he doesn't love us, he needs to protect his property.

Copin They want me to confess.

Rabbi Ben Barachyal What can you confess? Remember Copin, they cannot kill you!

Copin Rabbi, I'm frightened – they want a confession – any confession . . . they'll torture me!

Rabbi Ben Barachyal If you confessed they could kill you, even your wife and children too. A confession could excite the mob to attack us as they did in York.

Copin I'm a frail old man, Rabbi.

Rabbi Ben Barachyal For God's sake Copin, you must try not to make a false confession – I will try to persuade them from using torture.

Copin (*trembling*) I'm sick with fear that I'll confess when I see the rack.

Rabbi Ben Barachyal Would you rather die?

Copin Than face their inventions – anything.

Rabbi Ben Barachyal I could bring you in a phial of poison made by one of our physicians to take only when it's unendurable.

Copin (*surprised in spite of his fear*) Is that not a terrible thing for a Rabbi to do?

Rabbi Ben Barachyal To prevent something more terrible – God understands, but he would rather you did not take it.

Copin (*beginning to weep*) I'm so weak Rabbi, give me courage.

Rabbi Ben Barachyal (*gently*) Do you know that every man who suffers for Israel will find an honoured place for himself there, when the land becomes ours once again?

Copin A dream Rabbi – give me courage!

Rabbi Ben Barachyal (*desperately hoping he can*) In Trent, a learned man called Samuel was stripped naked, bound and drawn up high on a rope – the rope drops and was jerked up quickly to ease his joints from their sockets – they put boiled eggs under his armpits and set fire to his beard . . . Eventually at his own request he is burned at the stake as a personal favour.

Copin That courage I do not know.

Rabbi Ben Barachyal He found his courage on the rope – but they will do none of these things to you, Copin.

Copin That helps a bit – tell me more, Rabbi.

Rabbi Ben Barachyal Do you know about Hananiah – the teacher? He and his wife were condemned to death. They wrapped him in the holy scrolls and placing him on a pyre of green brush, set fire to it – his daughter watching was in despair. As he burns he says, 'I should despair if I alone were burned, but since the scrolls are burning with me, the power that avenges the offence against the law will avenge the offence against me.'

Copin (*suddenly overcome by a wave of fear*) Are you sure you can bring the poison to me – bring it now Rabbi – I may not be able to take it when it is unendurable . . .

Rabbi Ben Barachyal (*gripping Copin's hand as if he could force courage into him*) . . . After a while this same Hananiah was asked by his disciples what he sees and Hananiah replies – that he sees the parchment burning whilst the law flies up . . .

Copin Poison, Rabbi! . . . bring me poison, I'm no martyr.

Rabbi Ben Barachyal (*continuing desperately – hopelessly*) . . . His disciples whilst he was burning said,

'Open your mouth Rabbi' that the smoke may have choked off his life and spared him further suffering, and he said, 'No man may hasten his own death' . . . (*Silence.*) Anyway Copin – they will do none of these things to you.

Copin (*attempting to smile nervously*) Then what have I to fear! It's just that I'm a terrible coward . . . That kind of courage I do not possess.

Rabbi Ben Barachyal Courage comes to the righteous at the moment of need – you will soon be home – the Chief Rabbi is conferring with the King's brother at this moment, also an emissary is being sent to the Pope – we are not alone . . .

SCENE FOURTEEN

A meeting of the Jews a few hours later – the community's leading members are represented, including some financiers. Rabbi Ben Moses, who pleads moderation, is also there.

Isaac On the contrary, Rabbi, it would seem as if we were very much alone . . . so . . . a bribed Pope condemned these charges once – after our brethren were slaughtered in London, but who remembers, who cares – the world remembers the other Popes, the ones who weren't so partial.

First Financier For ten years it's been quiet, why should it start again?

Second Financier Why did it start before? – someone's coffers are getting low!

First Financier The last seven years the King has fined us seven times – our veins have been bled dry – after the infamous London charge we were poorer by 60,000 marks – must we keep paying for these filthy lies – when will it stop?

Rabbi Ben Moses It is an unfortunate expedient, but until we can leave this heartless country for ever, a necessary one – if we wish to leave it alive.

Second Financier Kings and Popes! So far this is only a local charge and by appealing to the Earl of Cornwall or the Pope – just the spreading of the fabricated charge will harm us – people will remember the charge and forget the fabrication – they want money – give it to them, give them their blood money – this is Lincoln, not London – they might not be so greedy.

Jacob No! – this must stop! – no more blood money.

Isaac Are you mad, Jacob?

Jacob Every time you pay this blood money you strengthen the legend – don't you see, there is no end – every time they want money they dangle a child's corpse in our faces and we dive into our pockets like frightened rabbits.

Rabbi Ben Moses Rather frightened rabbits than skinned ones, Jacob.

Jacob I am sick of your perpetual victim philosophy, Rabbi . . .

Rabbi Ben Moses Recently our Chief Rabbi Elias has twice begged the King to release us from this country to go to more clement shores – and twice the King has refused – one day we'll be so poor and destitute he will be forced to free us – until then we are subjected to his will.

Jacob Refuse to pay one mark – put ourselves on trial – prove once and for all that we are innocent of this charge – put a final end to it – Kill it! – we have the lawyers, we have witnesses – must we always meekly bend to the Christian whip?

First Financier (*sympathetically*) Our innocence is uninteresting when what motivates the charge is greed –

Jacob Must we always be hostages to their greed?

First Financier The Barons want money to fight the King – the King wants money to fight the crusades, and what are the crusades? An excuse for the Barons rampaging and killing Jews throughout Europe, collecting more money to fight the King – so what sense is your search for truth – the Rabbi is right – we pay till we get out – perhaps thin men, but live ones. We are buying time.

Jacob We could appeal to the Clergy . . . the Archbishop . . . (*laughter*) the Bishop of London . . . (*laughter*) to the Monks – there must be someone who would help us.

First Financier If there is you won't find him in the church!

Jacob The Pope!

First Financier Alas, were he nearer! In fact the King has often protected us from some of the more zealous members of the clergy – after all they are the power in this land – the King-makers.

Second Financier More than once the clergy furnished the evidence of our 'crimes' – recently they accused us of making away with a baptised child and circumcising him – the whole congregation of the town was thrown into prison and released only on heavy payment.

Isaac Nevertheless I feel that Jacob speaks sense – a trial would clear the air – whether our innocence is interesting or not to the Kings and Bishops, it would be to the people . . . Our usury is becoming dangerous – the Church condemns us the more it gets into our debt – the Barons accuse us of being royalist because we pay huge taxes to the King – whichever way we turn we are condemned.

Jacob We are condemned – condemned to live – condemned to move, condemned to die!

Second Financier (*with irony*) As Pope Innocent III said, 'We are doomed like the fratricide Cain to wander about the earth as fugitives and vagabonds and our faces must be covered with shame' . . . Poor Jacob, you are not yet used to it.

Jacob No – and never will be – we must learn something new . . . fighting back – the times are changing – we have been accepting our fate too easily – instead of paying blood money we should elect to spend it on the largest trial Lincoln has ever seen – bring experts from all over Europe to refute the charge – kill the vile stigma for the last time!

First Financier Innocent child – the charge cannot be refuted – it is written in their books that we killed God – that is the real charge – that is what unites the Christian hatred of us . . . These extra charges of crucifying children merely help to keep it alive, to whip up their flagging spirits, to extract money in times of troubles – it was always thus, and will be always thus – and if we kill the blood accusation charge they will find another – they will never be short of accusations to point at a Jew.

Silence for a moment.
The Franciscan Monk earlier seen in the church has crept in silently and is listening at the back.

Monk Ah – that is right, as you kill one charge another will be born – even from its corpse –

They turn round astonished.

– because you create them and feed them.

Congregation Get him out of here! – is he a spy? – what are you doing – who are you?

Monk My name is John Reding – I am a Franciscan.

Rabbi Ben Moses Who sent you here?

Monk I sent myself – there are some of us who wish to help you.

Reaction of scorn.

Voice Throw him out, he's a spy!

Monk (*continuing*) Why do you think they're bringing these charges – because they know you will pay – they have accepted your token of complicity – you both accept the monstrosity, so together you create the charge – do not accept it any more – do not pay! As you say, do not make yourselves hostages to greed.

Second Financier How easy for you to say that, Monk – what will they do to us? – imprison our wives and children – kill us? – we'd rather pay.

Monk Neither will they do that if you unite your entire forces and not give in.

Jacob Why are you so sure Monk?

Monk Because hitherto you enticed them to bring the ritual murder accusation on you by demonstrating how rich you would make them . . . Now if you had the courage to refuse paying one penny . . .

First Financier They would make bonfires of us all.

Monk They need you too much for that – the King is not unrealistic – he knows the Jews are crucial to the prosperity of the country.

Congregation laughs.

Isaac Could he not take our wealth anyway?

Monk Perhaps he could do that, but he would have no means to breed more money – since the Church forbids usury to Christians, he would be forced to use heathens who are not inhibited in charging exorbitant rates.

First Financier (*scornful*) What is sinful for Christians is alright for heathens . . . and Jews . . .

Monk (*smiling*) The Church realises that you're probably more honest in usury than our fellow Christians – also as I said you are essential – they may choose to punish some to see how far you will go in your refusal to pay, but they do this anyway even when you do pay.

Rabbi Ben Moses They may *punish* some of us!? Who is going to volunteer to be a martyr – we have given enough martyrs – God gave us one weapon – our mercantile skill – to soften the Christian fist, not to use this weapon would crush us utterly.

Jacob Rabbi – should we not try this once – just this one time refuse to pay any fine – force them to try us – make them understand that this is the last time they will rob us. If we dry up this source of money the rumour will also dry up and eventually die!

Rabbi Ben Moses Jacob – your father is in prison suffering what tribulation we do not know – would you be prepared to sacrifice him – to deny him his possible means of escape? (*Jacob is bewildered.*) Would you be prepared to see him tied to a stake with perhaps your mother at his side and who knows who else – could you look upon that?

Monk (*becoming enraged*) You must not walk around with one foot in the fire – you seem to expect punishment – you ask for it! . . . Reject it! You anticipate your

54

executioner and walk tamely to the stake! Reject it! Are you born with the seed of self-destruction, waiting your whole life for that moment – expecting it, no – driving yourself onto it – craving your martyrdom – then cast it out of you! Reject it!

Rabbi Ben Moses We do not seek martyrdom – it seeks us!

Monk It smells you out as cats do birds – the victim creates himself . . . Be not victims . . . Elect yourself for trial – hold your lives firmly in your hands – do not bargain for flesh.

Jacob (*becoming enthused*) Perhaps if we demanded a trial they would be afraid of harming my father before the outcome.

Congregation (*excited by the thought of an ally and charged by the Monk's fervour*) A trial! . . . a just one . . . no more fines, no more murders . . .

Monk How weak the dead boy's case is. How curious that the parents discovered, as did everyone else, special marks – crucifixion marks, one day *after* they found the body . . . why not when they found it!

Isaac He claimed he saw them straight away but did not understand what they were.

Monk Other people saw the body – they would know . . . No, their case is weak and yours is strong – the Franciscan Order is strongly supporting you – word has got to London where the accusation arouses great sympathy for you in certain quarters.

First Financier How far can they drive us before we break?

Monk Not as far as you think they can.

Isaac (*to congregation. A sense of excitement permeates the air as if at last they could change their fate – a sense of challenge*) How many of us are in agreement – to try this way – refuse to pay – not to countenance our guilt again – we are not alone any more!

> *Nearly everybody in the congregation raises their hand and there is much excitement and chatter. Just at this moment the heavy stooping figure of Rabbi Ben Barachyal enters. They all turn looking jubilant.*

Rabbi Ben Barachyal What! . . . Has the Messiah come?

Jacob (*looking elated*) We have news for you, Rabbi!

Rabbi Ben Baryachal Then let it follow mine so that it might sweeten the taste . . . Copin has confessed, that in league with various people he did seize little Hugh and did crucify him and cover him with thorns and use his blood for evil purposes . . . That is my news – now tell me yours, Jacob.

> *The Rabbi looks gravely at them. They all turn to look at the Monk as if he were somehow to blame – they feel tricked, deceived. One senses by their distraught faces that the Monk's idea now seems remote, too brave to risk.*

Act Two

SCENE FIFTEEN

Beatrice and Luke, the following day. Luke is drunk and in a surly mood.

Beatrice So what you going to do about it eh? Just sit there drinking yourself stupid?

Luke Pox on you – should I tell the Sheriff, 'Look here you've got 10,000 marks of silver out of them Jews, what about sharing it?' Ha, ha! He'd like me for that.

Beatrice Why not, if it weren't for us they would have got nought!

Luke Shut your nagging hole – he'll give me some.

Beatrice But he didn't say so, did he – he didn't actually tell you he would! Not in so many words.

Luke He ain't got it yet, has he – they're still trying to raise it – but they're not letting Copin go until they've got the fine money – and when they've got it we'll be looked after – don't you worry.

Beatrice If there's any left for us.

Luke There'll be plenty.

Beatrice What?! After Father Arnold's got his chunk there won't – and all the other vultures!

Luke You shouldn't be saying that – that's holy money for the church.

Beatrice That's what they tell oafs like you . . . (*Silence. She stares into a wealthy future which seems to be*

57

evading her.) Ten thousand silver marks . . . what we could do with some of that, eh Luke?

Luke We got something out of it – we got no more debts and a bit over beside.

Beatrice A bit! We could have been rich – really rich for once – after all we did . . .

Luke (*mean*) All *I* did you scab – I had to do it all, didn't I – I've had nightmares ever since, digging up his poor grave and doing all that . . . Oh it was a dreadful thing I did Beatrice – I keep seeing that coffin poking through the earth that morning – that was an evil omen – we're cursed for sure!

Beatrice Oh don't talk that old woman's rot – you were so drunk you didn't put it back properly and the rain all night opened the earth.

Luke (*hopefully*) You think that's true Beatrice, I mean you *really* think that – you're not just saying it?

Beatrice I told you that was the reason – anyway it made them believe it all the more didn't it – so what you worried about?

Luke Maybe they don't really believe us – maybe they know.

Beatrice How they going to know that eh? You going to tell them?

Luke Why are they letting Copin go then when they've got their fine money? – that means they're still not bloody sure otherwise he'd be at the stake for that kind of crime. (*quickly*) Now that's true isn't it – but they're letting him go.

Beatrice For a large price they are, for which we're getting nought.

Edmund during this has been listening behind door.

Luke A large price, but they're still letting him go – and he'll be living in this town, walking around, knowing that we did it – he and the others will know and maybe one day they'll find out how it happened – they're cunning, they'll find out.

Beatrice But he confessed, didn't he – you can't change that.

Luke Wouldn't any man on the rack? (*fearfully*) Oh God – if they ever put me on the rack where would I find the strength to deny what I did.

Beatrice (*angry*) You're feverish – nobody's putting you on the rack.

Luke If only the earth would swallow him up – I couldn't look Copin in the face again – no, none of them . . . Maybe we should get out of Lincoln . . . I don't like all this Bea . . .

Beatrice (*suddenly worried*) You're right – they shouldn't really let him go – not if they really believed – they should tie him to the stake down the square and burn him – that's what they should do.

Luke (*worried*) There, you see – you don't like it either!

Beatrice (*Luke's uncertainty affecting her*) The whole lot of them with their magic crafts and evil doings and all the money they squeeze out of us poor, making *them* rich – living in big houses with ermine fur coats and pearls on their fingers . . . They should burn the lot! (*becoming excited*) A huge fire in the square and watch them squirming on their stakes with the scorch of their roasting bodies filling the town . . .

Luke (*catching her excitement*) Like they did in London when Richard was crowned.

Beatrice That's right – I remember my old mother telling me about that. What a time they had (*laughing amiably at the memory*) Apparently the Crusaders were that keen to get rid of them that they burnt part of the city as well! (*suddenly thinking of some old affair*) Oh they were rogues those Crusaders . . . (*thoughtfully again*) But they shouldn't let him go – not for doing those kind of things to little innocent children, like they do – that's a kind of monster that is . . . fancy doing that . . . and drinking his blood and all – that's witchcraft. (*Starts weeping.*) Oh poor little Hugh.

Luke (*confused*) But they didn't do it did they – you'll start believing yourself soon!

Beatrice But it's almost as if they did – I feel they *did* do it – 'cause they done it before – Father Arnold says it's what they do . . .

Luke (*disturbed*) Maybe it is and maybe it isn't.

Beatrice What! Are you contradicting the Holy Father?

Luke I'm just saying they didn't do it to ours – that's what I'm saying – when you can't separate between what you say and what you do – that's a sign of your wits crumbling.

Beatrice (*shouting, not wanting to feel guilty, needing her belief in the crime to sustain her*) But Father Arnold said . . .

Luke (*interrupting*) Oh shut it with what he said! You're like a parrot – you'd jump in the lake if he said it was good for you.

Beatrice (*silenced for a moment*) I'll tell the King!

Luke (*astounded*) I told you – your wits really are crumbling!

Beatrice He's passing through Lincoln in the morning –
I'll ask to see him.

Luke (*alarmed*) You can't see the King! You're mad!
What will that do?

Beatrice It will show them that we don't want murderers
let loose with their filthy gold – I'll tell him that! – Oh
Luke, maybe we'll have our fires after all and you won't
have to worry no more.

Luke is completely bewildered.

Eh, Luke? Come on . . . Come here to me.

He seems quite stunned.

Come on . . . hold me Luke. (*She puts his arms round
her.*) Come on Luke – like you used to . . . you don't
hold me any more.

He vaguely obeys her instructions.

Now tighter, Luke . . . really tight!

SCENE SIXTEEN

*Chambers of Henry III the following day. He is with a
priest and his advisor.*

Beatrice (*sobbing a little as she recounts the story*) He
was such a *gentle* little boy – he wouldn't have harmed a
tiny fly, and I've got another one – oh he's so sweet too –
just like his brother and I think – suppose it were to
happen again! I couldn't bear the thought – if it
happened once, it could happen again and maybe to
one of mine again . . . (*She bursts into tears.*)

King Rest assured good woman it shall not happen
again. (*He signals for her to be escorted out.*) Ten

thousand silver marks – greedy little Lexington – thinks to make some capital for himself.

Advisor The last case in London cost them sixty thousand marks.

King Sixty thousand, by God! – Is that how much we got – remind me of that one?

Advisor A body of a boy was found in the graveyard of St Paul's Cathedral with ritual cuts.

King Oh yes! I remember – of course London's a much bigger city – they couldn't find that money here.

Advisor Nevertheless Aaron of York found 30,000 silver marks besides 200 marks of gold for her Majesty – and York is no larger than Lincoln.

King So you think they should pay more?

Advisor That would depend on the strength of the case.

Priest Your Highness, it would be indeed a blessing if the valiant Knights gathering in London for the crusade against Jerusalem were to benefit from this.

King It would, would it? . . .

Priest Oh yes, your Highness – to what better cause could the money go? They have mortgaged their land, their houses, even their cattle, indeed they are hard-pressed . . .

King Hmmn! I'm not able to help them! – I can't even raise enough money for my own armies for the wars at home with the Barons.

Priest (*persisting*) It would be tragic if the wresting of Jerusalem from the Turks should be met with failure after all their bloody attempts – one Knight had to sell his wife . . .

King Then they will have to make another bloody attempt – even Richard the Lion Heart couldn't take it.

Priest But he would have been so proud if the Holy City were taken by his nephew.

King (*becoming enraged*) Let the Earl of Cornwall go – let Simon de Montfort go – they're richer than I am, aren't they! My brother owns the lead mines in Cornwall, let them take the cross to the Holy Land – I've got a country to run.

Priest (*unsubtly*) So had King Richard.

King When did he run a country – the only time he came here was to finance himself for his Palestine adventures . . . He mortgaged the country to the Barons and he would have sold London had he found a buyer – so now the land is bustling with rebellion – I don't even own the Jews any more . . . I am as poor as a church mouse – if you want money go and see dear brother Richard. (*Becomes maddened, takes priest by the scruff.*) Go on, get out of here with your begging bowl. (*Throws him out.*) I am sick of being compared with my uncle . . .

Advisor You can *still* own the Jews.

King How can I do that when I've pledged them to Cornwall?

Advisor (*reads from a book of statutes*) 'If any Jew be arrested for a criminal offence his money, land and property are confiscate to the Crown.'

King Show me that! (*He reads. An expression of joy comes over his face.*) How is it I didn't know this before?

Advisor This is the first case since you sold them.

King Aah! So – John of Lexington thinks to line his purse at my expense.

Advisor Furthermore the guilt of all the Jews here is explicit by their bribing Lexington.

King How is that?

Advisor Obviously the man Copin couldn't find such a vast sum – they're forced to solicit from others – therefore they are all implicated.

King Better and better! Good, let Sheriff John come in now.

A guard goes to fetch him.

How wonderful! (*Bursts into wild laughter.*) I can just see Cornwall's face when I tell him . . .

Advisor There is nothing he can do except protest!

Sheriff enters.

King Sheriff John, forgive us for making you wait . . . Ah yes, about this Beatrice Tanner.

Sheriff John We have thoroughly investigated the case – the woman has no grounds for alarm or for disturbing you.

King She complains that you are to release the Jew – killer of her child.

Sheriff John The woman is itching with greed – that is her only concern – she will do anything for gold.

King There is many a man who will do anything for gold as well, Sheriff John – but why release him?

Sheriff John (*pretending not to notice slight*) They were determined not to pay a penny without assurances that Copin's life would be spared – they are also supported by the Franciscans. Had we executed Copin we might have got far less.

King Why were they so determined – the Jew usually pays without demands?

Sheriff John They said that they had been bled so much with taxes that their condition was worse than their ancestors under the Pharaohs – they seemed determined to hold out.

King Did they indeed – and you were bullied by their threats?

Sheriff John I would love to see these Christ-killers burned as much as the next man, your Majesty, but I didn't want to risk losing the fine money, which is so badly needed here – besides there was an element of doubt.

King There seems to be none in the woman's mind.

Sheriff John At the time of the boy's death the Jews were celebrating a wedding – Lincoln saw the leading Jews of their tribe from all parts of England gathered here . . . It made me doubt that they'd perform this act which they frequently do at Easter, while celebrating a wedding. Even the devil must rest.

Advisor Your Majesty –

> *Signals to King – he wishes to talk privately. They walk to one side.*

This could be the most incredible opportunity – since the leading Jews in England were here at the time, each one representing a particular community, they would all be guilty in concert of arranging this crime . . . In fact, this is probably what they gathered here for, under the *guise* of a wedding so as to divert suspicion.

King Incredible indeed! Carry on!

Advisor Then one could say that each particular community who elected its representative to be here were also guilty, and subject to punishment.

King (*seeing the vast potential*) Ah!

Advisor Therefore if we let one fish off the hook, we lose the shoal!

King I see the wisdom and the wit of it.

Advisor You could say the entire Jewish treasure of the country was represented here and you have the perfect opportunity to take it – legally.

King What about the Pope – he's getting greedy again for more money for his holy war against Frederick II?

Advisor Let him get it out of the clergy – tell him you need it for your own wars . . . holy and otherwise.

King The opportunity is golden.

Advisor Exactly! Also you weaken the Barons' grip.

King By arresting their money lenders!

Advisor Not only that – their debts will be transferred to you and as half the Barons are in the Jews' debt you'll have them by the throat.

King You're sure my brother can do nothing?

Advisor Not once you've proved Copin's guilt, plus the Jews' involvement, therefore Copin *must* be destroyed.

King Hmmn . . .

They return to Sheriff.

Sheriff John – we are disturbed that you should contemplate releasing this man, particularly in the face

66

of a confession . . . The wedding you described was obviously to disguise their real intentions – which was to sacrifice a Christian child according to their traditional beliefs – therefore the Jew Copin must be executed.

Sheriff John (*seeing his fine disappear*) This is unwise, your Majesty.

King For whom, Sheriff John?

Sheriff John (*knows he is lost – cynically*) How would your Majesty like him put to death?

King Have him dragged round the streets naked, tied to the tail of a horse and then hang him for all to see . . . Then arrest every Jew in Lincoln and make conveyances for them to be transported to the Tower. (*to advisor*) You'll send soldiers to every town which sent a representative to the ritual and arrest the entire Hebrew population. Secondly, obtain the debt chests before the Barons destroy them – that's *very* important. (*aside to advisor*) As soon as the Barons hear of the money-lenders' arrest their debt records will be the first thing they'll attempt to destroy.

Advisor smiles at King. Sheriff looks at both in astonishment.

SCENE SEVENTEEN

Assembly of bishops and priests at the local parish fighting over Hugh's body.

Arnold But can you deny that the child was martyred within the precincts of the parish and laid to rest here . . . that his very gore brought sight to a blind man?

Archbishop No one is denying these facts, but for the greater glory of Lincoln it is only right that Hugh's remains be re-interred within the grounds of Lincoln Cathedral where the population of the country can do him proper homage.

Arnold (*seething*) But the child received his baptism here in this very font!

Archbishop Notwithstanding, it is the Archbishop of Canterbury's wish as well as ours that Hugh be blessed with Sainthood and laid to rest in hallowed ground with the other blessed Saints of Lincoln.

Father Arnold remains glaring at him.

SCENE EIGHTEEN

Luke and Beatrice later that night.

Luke (*in a semi-hysterical state*) Oh! You were going to be the fine woman of Lincoln with your furs and gold. Now what did your greed get you – nothing!

Beatrice We'll be rewarded plenty Luke, don't you worry!

Luke Oh yes! (*screams out laughing*) The King will give you plenty thanks for filling his coffers – he'll make you a Lady-in-Waiting to the Queen.

Beatrice He might at that.

Luke You greedy hag – now he's confiscated every mark the Jews got, I won't even have some of the fine money – he's taken that too!

Beatrice You wouldn't have got that – you said yourself you weren't promised.

Luke Don't tell me nothing – there was at least a chance we'd get something – now what we got, eh? Ah you stupid bitch – that ugly hole of yours will be the death of us yet.

Beatrice (*becoming tearful*) Don't Luke! Don't say no more – I can't stand your scorn any more – I only did what I thought was best.

Luke Oh did you – and what's the Sheriff going to say about this, not forgetting Father Arnold for the favour you did them, eh? You've made Lincoln poor, that's what you've done and every soul's going to thank *you* for that.

Beatrice No more Luke, please! I'll go out of my mind – stop it!

Luke Why? You started it with your sick greed . . . like a witch you are – making me do evil things I never thought I was capable of.

Beatrice (*screaming*) Nobody made you . . . you did it! You wanted to do it too – you started the rumour!

Luke (*flaring*) I did! You wanted a little martyr, you filthy beast, so everyone might think you're touched with a bit of holiness – don't say I started no rumour, woman.

Beatrice (*remorseful*) Oh Luke I'm ill with it all – hold me Luke, come here and hold me, I'm so unhappy.

Luke Oh get off me – go and put your arms round the corpse hanging in the square – you got what you wanted – go on – put your arms round him!

Beatrice If you don't stop it Luke, I'll tell them – I'll tell them what you did – how he fell down the well . . . I'll tell them everything if you don't leave it alone . . .

Luke (*a maniacal gleam in his eye, softly*) Go on then – tell them – go hang yourself!

Beatrice I will Luke, don't make me!

Luke Well, get on with it then – tell the town what a witch you are.

Beatrice (*moves to door*) I will!

Luke senses that in her hysteria she might say something – rushes to the door – hits her and drags her down to the floor. Takes out a large knife.

Luke My stomach is full of you, woman – you make one sound more or leave this house, I'll put this knife right through your belly!

From the next room Edmund has been watching – he now rushes in sobbing and screaming.

Edmund Oh Dad, don't do that! Please don't – don't hurt Ma, don't hurt her. (*He throws himself protectively around his mother.*)

SCENE NINETEEN

A mass of Jews are assembled in a series of dungeons in the Tower – there is much moaning and wailing. Rabbi Ben Barachyal and the monk are conversing in a small ante-room.

Monk Rabbi Barachyal, I beg you to offer yourselves for trial – the King has today ordered the execution of eighteen of your brethren for refusing to trust themselves to a Christian jury – whatever happens, you cannot help yourself in here.

Rabbi Ben Barachyal We appreciate your good solicitations, but we are condemned already – our trial merely gives them satisfaction of the legality of their murder – we do not wish to give them that – let them kill us like the base murderers they are.

Monk Our Order has made great protestations to the King – the Earl of Cornwall and the Archbishop – you're not condemned yet . . . also they have selected me to defend you when you face trial.

Rabbi Ben Barachyal (*amazed*) You to defend us?

Monk Yes, the examination will be conducted by an apostate Jew and a lawyer – you are allowed a non-Jew to assist you plus one of your representatives – therefore I suggest that you and I prepare our cases immediately.

Rabbi Ben Barachyal Brother John – we are not afraid to aid the murderers. (*softly*) You have brought what I asked?

Monk Yes.

Rabbi Ben Barachyal Then you will give it to me?

Monk (*taking out two large knives*) Why do you wish them, Rabbi?

Rabbi Ben Barachyal As I said Brother John – there is a man in need of surgery and our physician has no tools – do not be alarmed, we shall not attempt to hack our way out of the Tower with these!

Monk Think swiftly, Rabbi – a trial would be of more good than rotting in the Tower.

Rabbi Ben Barachyal We shall see, we shall see . . . Goodbye Brother John.

Monk exits. Voices come from the dark recesses as if disembodied.

First Voice So what does he say, Rabbi? The King begs our forgiveness?

Second Voice Quiet all of you!

Third Voice Are you mad to say such things without asking about our brethren taken from us?

Fourth Voice Where are they Rabbi – where are they?

Rabbi Ben Barachyal (*simply*) Our eighteen brethren who were taken from us yesterday are now in a far happier place, watching down on us and eager for us to join them.

>   *Series of gasps and screams from the friends and relatives, clanking and banging of doors, tears and wailing.*

Fifth Voice God is also dead!!

Rabbi Ben Barachyal (*he has remained in the same position the monk left him in, as if he cannot face the voices behind him*) Do not despair children – many years ago in York, Rabbi Yomtob and his flock had barricaded themselves in a fortress, defending themselves against the crusading spirit of the town. He said to them when they could hold out no longer . . . 'God commands us at this time to die for his law and behold, death is even before our eyes, and there is nothing left us to consider but how to undergo it in the most honourable manner . . . If we fall into the hands of our enemies our deaths will be cruel and ignominious – they will not only torment us, but despitefully use us – my advice therefore is that we voluntarily surrender our lives to our creator, which he seems to call for, and not wait for the executioners ourselves' . . . Our ancestors have proceeded in like manner on similar occasions.

>   *For the first time the Rabbi turns round and holds up high in the air the two knives . . . For a moment there is a terrible silence and the full implication sinks in.*

Voice of Jacob No Rabbi – let us make them kill us – make them work hard to destroy us – let us greedily hold on to the last drops of life . . . I implore you – make them crush us, so hard it will be to kill us – let's make them try us – since we are condemned anyway what matters what we say – let us speak our true minds for the first time – MAKE THEM KNOW US!!

SCENE TWENTY

Luke enters rather drunk – there is no one else there. He seems in a state of great tension. He wanders around humming for a moment. He sits down very carefully and takes out a handkerchief carefully folded over. He very delicately moves the cloth until it is a square with the long wafer on it. He looks at it for some time, then he carefully picks it up – examining it gingerly – holding it up – smelling it – he puts it down. He then takes out a knife. He wants to test Arnold's story not just out of curiosity but because he is tormented by guilt over what he has done and like Beatrice needs justification even at the risk of staining his own hands. He holds the wafer as if to stab it when a wave of fear makes him drop it – he lets out a shriek and shrinks back from the wafer – he's trembling. Gradually he goes back to the wafer, picks up the knife, but just looks at the wafer for some time – it might be a poisonous snake – very slowly, almost painfully he brings the knife in contact with the wafer but just touches it – he scrapes the surface.

Luke Forgive me Jesus, forgive me, but I've got to know . . .

He's enchanted and puts the knife back on the table and reflects.

Go on then, let me see . . .

Suddenly in a split second he stabs it – letting out a shout – and closes his eyes and darts away. Gradually he opens his eyes and returns to the wafer, which has split with the knife still in the table. His expression shows immense relief that he didn't cause it to bleed, followed by a sense of alarm that this like the other stories is false and he has countenanced a terrible crime.

Go on then, bleed, bleed, I want to see it! Bleed you bastard!

He takes knife up and continues stabbing, groaning with frustration and doubt.

SCENE TWENTY-ONE

The trial. A large court chamber where a representative group of Jews sits on one side and the jury composed of twelve Knights on the other side. In the centre the two opposing factions face each other. The King sits with friends in a spectators' box on the balcony.

Prosecutor *(a priest)* This year at the time of the Apostles Peter and Paul, the Jews of Lincoln stole a boy called Hugh who was eight years old. After shutting him in a secret chamber they fed him on milk and other childish foods, they sent to almost all the cities in England in which there were Jews and summoned them to be present at a sacrifice to take place at Lincoln in insult of Jesus Christ . . . They appointed a Jew of Lincoln judge to take place of Pilate, and on his concurrence the boy was subject to various tortures . . . They scourged him till the blood flowed, crowned him with thorns, mocked him and spat at him, each of them also pierced him with a knife and they made him drink gall – scoffed at him with blasphemous insults and kept gnashing their teeth and calling him Jesus – the false prophet – And then they crucified him, piercing his heart with a spear . . . When the boy was dead they disembowelled him – it is said for the purpose of their magic arts . . . On arrest the Jew whose name was Copin, thinking his gold would afford him means of escape, answered, 'If you will repay my words with deeds I will show wondrous things to you.' The wise John of Lexington encouraged him and the Jew confessed that what the Christians say is true . . . Almost every year the Jews crucify a boy in injury and insult to Jesus, using his blood for Passover biscuits, and many Jews are chosen to be present at the Pascal offering.

Judge One of you may speak in answer to what has been stated, but no more.

Rabbi Ben Barachyal (*stands*) The time of the Apostles Peter and Paul does not coincide with our Passover which happens months earlier, therefore we could not have made a Pascal sacrifice at the time – apart from this it is strictly forbidden in our law to shed human blood for sacrifice or to take it in any form . . .

In the Talmud it is said that if a drop of blood is found in an egg it cannot be eaten, it must be thrown away . . . before meat is eaten it must be washed, covered abundantly with salt and washed again . . . if you had studied our Torah you would find that the partaking of even animal blood is forbidden again and again . . . Our great teacher Malmonides has declared that whoever eats blood to the amount of an olive, risks the punishment of extirpation.

Second Prosecutor (*rising*) We have studied your Torah, Rabbi, and find that the consumption of human blood is not expressly forbidden . . . We challenge you to give one instance where it is. (*He sits.*)

Rabbi Ben Barachyal The lack of an expressed pronouncement concerning human blood is very simple – firstly, it is altogether beyond the imagination of the Israelite prophets to conceive that anyone would desire to partake of human blood.

Scornful laughter from opposition.

Secondly, human sacrifices are strictly prohibited in Leviticus and Deuteronomy.

Second Prosecutor Come now Rabbi, does not your God constantly demand blood – blood at his altar – blood at his feast, the sprinkling of blood on the doorposts of your houses on Passover . . . even your patriarch Abraham was to sacrifice his son Isaac, but this was too much even for your God, and so he made him stay his hand. Isaiah charges the Jews with 'inflaming themselves with idols under every green tree, slaying the children in the valley under the cliffs of the rocks' . . . Your altars have smoked with human blood from the time of Abraham and your Rabbinism is a full and swelling stream of corrupt doctrines and practices stretching back to your debased Zoroastrianism . . . And yet you talk of the 'blood of an egg'!

Rabbi Ben Barachyal (*simply*) The sacrificial lamb commemorates the delivery of Israel from the tyrannical Egyptians . . . Isaiah condemned the Caanites who sacrificed their firstborn to placate their God – in fact Gentiles used to bury human beings alive under new houses to ward off the devil . . . certainly Isaiah condemned these things – perhaps you haven't read our Torah well.

Second Prosecutor Well enough, Rabbi! . . . if I do not penetrate into it with passionate zeal it is because I smell the smells and remain aloof.

Judge Whilst this debate may be relevant to the case, would you be more specific – it is for the murder of Hugh the Jews are on trial, not for drinking blood.

Second Prosecutor I will show that these two acts are inseparable – but let us look at their past crimes leading up to this . . . In England alone, apart from France and Germany, they have been condemned. In 1160 Harold of Gloucester – crucified . . . In 1181 . . . Bury St Edmunds, sacrifice at Passover 1192, Winchester, crucifixion . . . 1232 also in Winchester . . . 1235 in Norwich they performed the foul act of circumcision on a Christian child . . . 1244, London, a child found with ritual cuts, and now Lincoln . . . These crimes have been following a steady pattern – who knows how many children have *not* been discovered . . . The wretch Copin who was hanged confessed, they say, only under torture . . . But even so, no torture could wring from an innocent man the details, the methods of cutting and the situation of the wounds! . . . Let us finally expose these methods of Jewish intrigue and malevolence.

Monk (*rises*) It is very disturbing that an act which has been so condemned by Pope Innocent IV should still find credence in this country.

First Prosecutor (*interrupting*) The views of Pope Innocent IV should not be misinterpreted. Only three years before the Papal Bull on ritual murder, namely in 1244, Pope Innocent IV showed plainly what he thought of the Talmud by pressing Louis IX to collect all the copies of the Talmud and assign them to the flames!

Monk (*exasperated*) I suppose the Pope can be as susceptible to poisoned ideas as the next man.

First Prosecutor To poisoned ideas never – the Pope is infallible – your statements are growing blasphemous.

Monk And it is gratifying to see that he issued this Papal Bull *after* having condemned the Talmud as if in remorse for what he did – I also note that in none of these cases mentioned by the accusers was there a trial, and that popular rumour was considered sufficient to establish the martyrdom of the lads . . . And prove a considerable source of attraction, financial and otherwise, to the cathedrals and abbeys of these towns –

Strong reaction.

– that this is in fact the first trial, the first time the Jews have elected to fight this perfidious charge, and it shall be fought with truth and science – against the vile accusations and pagan superstitions nourished by the darker sides of Christendom!

First Prosecutor Are you an apostate, Monk, that you criticise your own faith? . . . You are not here for that reason but to defend the Jewish faith in what way that is possible . . . If Pope Innocent IV did not outrightly condemn Jews of this charge it is because Christian charity inhibited his zeal. But no such inhibition deterred our righteous Innocent III who condemned them time and time again – who confirmed this charge of ritual murder – who threatened excommunication on any Christian who had dealings with the Jews – who condemned Princes for protecting them – who grieved that the very wine used for the sacrament of the Lord's Supper was made by Jewish wine merchants – whose hope of your final conversion to the true path was the only thought that prevented His Holiness from declaring a war of extermination on you – (*pointing to Rabbi*) who even condemned you to wearing the badge you are wearing now as your mark of Cain . . . So do not dare to speak, Brother John, of the Pope's tolerance of such a crime. Remember Isaiah's prophecy, 'Humiliated thou shalt speak upon the ground . . . and from the dust thy lips shall lisp.'

SCENE TWENTY-TWO

The trial. A day has passed, the passage of time shown in signs of fatigue and dishevelment. The heat is unbearable. Several knights are asleep.

First Prosecutor . . . It was disputed yesterday that their Jewish book ever demanded the drinking of blood, yet in their vile act of circumcision it is plainly seen that their God YAHWEH demands the shedding of blood and the mutilation of innocent babes. (*Shows a cup.*) This cup is known as a *mezizah* – it is used for storing the blood shed by the child and was probably used in the case of Hugh . . . The Rabbi after having used the slaughterer's knife on the child's organ and deformed it, then sucks the blood from the wound and mixes it with wine which is then drunk during their Passover feasts when Christian blood is not available . . . The act is so heinous as almost to defy description . . .

Rabbi stands immediately.

Rabbi Ben Barachyal This is such a misreading, it is unanswerable!

First Prosecutor (*quickly*) Down Rabbi, I have not finished yet.

Judge signals Rabbi to be seated.

Furthermore for the healing of the wound caused by the ritual act, they again use blood, which is made into a gum for the purpose of sealing the wound – commonly known as *calamus draco* or dragon's blood . . . rather a suitable description!

Rabbi Ben Barachyal May I now speak?

Judge You may.

Rabbi Ben Barachyal We are being condemned on such a misreading of our books that I cannot defend something which is not even stated – not only have we been condemned, but murdered by the very imperfect knowledge that Christians have of our religion and customs . . . Circumcision is a covenant between Abraham and God which symbolises a purification of his son, when instead of slaying him he made the sacrifice of his foreskin. The wine the Rabbi uses is to protect the wound from disease and the wound if not sucked out would be dangerous to the child's life . . . The will of God desires his people to obey his commandment . . . As the prophets say, 'Circumcise even the foreskin of your heart' – it means to purify and to cleanse.

First Prosecutor You are saying then that all Christians are unclean are you not, for not being circumcised?

Rabbi Ben Barachyal I am saying that we are not guilty of sacrificing Hugh of Lincoln or any other Christian child – that is what I am saying.

First Prosecutor But you are inferring that we are unclean?

Rabbi Ben Barachyal (*in difficulties*) Ishmael too was circumcised, it is not wholly a Jewish rite.

First Prosecutor You do not answer the question correctly, Rabbi – you infer that we are unclean – we Christians – not Israelites, not Saracens, not Muslims – us!

Rabbi Ben Barachyal (*faltering*) Circumcision is a mark of our loyalty to God – it is a mark by which he may recognise us.

First Prosecutor Would you say that all men are made in God's image, Rabbi?

Rabbi Ben Barachyal It is said.

First Prosecutor Therefore you would be saying that God is circumcised?

Rabbi Ben Barachyal God is absolute unity – he is not a corporeal being – he is invisible to us – form and matter and ideas are within him, and it is through his will that we are created – therefore man is created in his image – the image within his will.

First Prosecutor Unconvincing, Rabbi – you hide yourself behind a wood of metaphysics and sophistry . . . I bring you facts . . . (*picking up a book*) This will prove beyond all doubt your belief in blood shedding; this diary of a Jew-physician to King Richard of England reveals that when King Richard was suffering from leprosy he said to him – 'I know of a powerful remedy if your Majesty had heart enough to employ it . . . Know you that you will recover your health completely if you can make up your mind to bathe in the blood of a newborn child – but because the remedy is external, it must be helped out by an additional recipe to remove the inward root of the malady . . . Namely, the child's heart must be added, which your Majesty must eat and consume quite warm and raw, just as it has been taken from the body . . . ' This is fact, Rabbi, not abstract word-juggling.

> *Rabbi and Monk look disturbed. The jury look convinced. The leatherbound diary is passed around. The King peers over his box.*

Monk May we see the diary?

> *It is passed to them. Rabbi and Monk confer together and then Rabbi smiles.*

First Prosecutor Our learned Rabbi finds this horror amusing?

Rabbi Ben Barachyal No Jewish physician wrote this monstrosity – it is bound in the hide of a pig!

He hands it back to them and sits. Two prosecutors look alarmed and examine diary.

First Prosecutor (*upset*) The physician was obviously not concerned with your magic taboos when binding his books.

Rabbi Ben Barachyal But obviously he was – otherwise he would not recommend that old taboo first instigated by the Egyptian Pharaoh who bathed in the blood of the children of Israel to cure himself of leprosy.

Court in some confusion.

SCENE TWENTY-THREE

Another part of the building. The two prosecutors, advisor and King.

King How much longer?

First Prosecutor The case against them is already tight – very tight – only cracks need to be sealed before they are suffocated.

King The longer it goes on the more difficult it becomes – I am constantly besieged on their behalf – I have had messengers from the Pope, who is not convinced – we must convince them.

Second Prosecutor We are doing so, your Majesty.

King I could see that today – where do you dig up your facts – are they not glaring at you? Diaries of unknown physicians! My uncle Richard never had leprosy in his life, you dolts! – don't you ever check your evidence? . . . I had to listen to this drivel and keep quiet – whilst you slowly let those greasy Jews slide out of your grip . . . Richard died of his wounds. (*suddenly*) Leprosy being contagious could have transferred itself to me, therefore the people may soon think I carry it within me – you stupid imbeciles – what have you done?

Advisor The point was disproved, though, your Majesty . . .

King (*raging*) I don't care! It was mentioned – it was breathed – a calumny that may grow – 'It is said his uncle was a leper'. . . . You know how legends grow – look at the . . . (*Stops himself short – feels awkward, so becomes angry.*) Listen carefully, I shall end the trial tomorrow – and if the Jews are not roundly condemned there may be two others who will find themselves hanging instead – now get out!

Two prosecutors exit.

Advisor And if the trial is not resolved tomorrow?

King Of no consequence – I must hang them – the pressure is too great – the Barons are uniting to march on Gloucester – I need every penny I can get. Simon de Montfort, the traitor, is opposing me too and joining them – the situation is severe – I must have their money!

Advisor You will be destroying a rich vein of money if you hang them – the Church still will forbid any but Jews to practise usury . . . Destroy them and you destroy your means of milking both the Clergy and the Barons who borrow from them.

King I should let a few go?

Advisor Certainly – fine them heavily, but leave them

enough to start again – let them grow wealthy and then when the fruit is ripe cut it off. That way you will be thought clement by the Pope – your brother will be less offended – the Barons will not feel the knife at their throats as they would if their debts were in your hands – also history will record you as a forgiving and kindly King . . .

King (*smiles*) Hmmn . . .

SCENE TWENTY-FOUR

The trial, the following day.

Second Prosecutor . . . So stupid is this hysterical shriek, 'Our laws do not permit it,' that I will admit without further investigation of the Jewish laws that they are right.

Strong reaction from court at this apparent volte-face.

Ritual murder is contrary to their laws . . . Now is it likely that we would find sanction for this crime *written*, for the world to witness? . . . Of course not, or they would have perished were it so blatantly prescribed. But this does not mean that they do not do it. We know that according to Jewish belief the *ger* or stranger, in fact all those not belonging to their religion, are considered brute beasts so that what we call *murder* is only slaughter to them . . . As I have said, the Talmud declares that there are two kinds of blood pleasing to the Lord (a) the Pascal holocaust, (b) that of circumcision. What sort of people is this whose God finds the blood of human genitals pleasing?! . . . We have shown that Papal authority has condemned them time and again for this crime – they have been condemned from Socrates in ancient Greece to the present . . . Theobald of Cambridge, himself a convert to Christianity, has confirmed the general conspiracy and who should know better than one of their own . . . Did they not call out to Pilate when they crucified our dear Jesus in the same way as they crucified innocent Hugh, '*His blood be upon us and upon our children*' – that this curse is eternally on them? That in revenge for their scattered state they seek nourishment in murdering our young. Of course their book does not sanction ritual murder – the murder of the Messiah is not even there – does it mean that *he* does not exist? Or would you say that his crucifixion was an invention, Rabbi, or would you, Brother John, claim it to be a product of the darker side of Christendom?

Monk (*rising, deliberately ignoring his last comments*) I am glad that the Council for the Crown has decided that there is no justification in Jewish law for the crime the entire Jewish nation is absurdly accused of . . . this is indeed progress . . . Hitherto he was declaring that justification existed amply in their books.

Second Prosecutor I've given you the reason why it couldn't exist!

Monk Thank you.

Second Prosecutor (*grimly*) In their books I mean to say! It amply exists outside of them! . . . You do not, or cannot answer my last question.

Monk I thought it rhetorical – forgive me . . . would you repeat it?

Second Prosecutor (*becoming exasperated*) Because they do not keep a record of their crimes, beginning with Our Lord, which is nowhere found in their books – this does not mean he does not exist!

Monk Of course not – he is so well documented in our own books.

Second Prosecutor (*beginning to boil*) You still do not answer properly.

Rabbi Ben Barachyal (*rising*) Excuse me, but for what are we on trial?

Judge It is not your turn to speak.

Rabbi Ben Barachyal I should like to know!

Judge (*to Monk*) Would you please restrain your colleague.

Monk Please Rabbi, you may answer his questions soon.

First Prosecutor Is the Rabbi offering insult to the Court by such a question?

Monk I understand the Rabbi to mean whether they are on trial for Christ's execution or the so-called execution of Hugh – I feel that the learned Prosecutor's case, becoming weaker, seeks to plunge into history in order to strengthen it. (*He sits.*)

First Prosecutor On the contrary we wish to show how history and the present go hand in hand.

Rabbi Ben Barachyal (*standing*) I cannot begin to defend us for a crime reputed to us 1200 years ago, but I can only say it is as much a fallacy as the present one!

Second Prosecutor (*leaps up delightedly*) Would you therefore admit, rephrasing your sentence a little, that you are as guilty of Hugh's death as you are of Christ's?

Rabbi Ben Barachyal (*weary, no longer concerned with the arguments, accusations, the fine points of law, simply wanting it over. Sees it as a hopeless, biased piece of chicanery*) As you say – we are as guilty of Hugh's death as of Christ's.

86

Uproar and reaction.

Judge Careful Rabbi – you are condemning yourself out of your own mouth.

Rabbi Ben Barachyal (*indifferent*) Are we not condemned anyway – do you not seek to martyr us in celebration of your Christ's agony – have you not done so regularly with fervour for a crime which did not even exist, but was as much an invention as the multifarious other crimes that have been attributed to us through the ages? . . . A Jewish court could not have passed sentence of crucifixion without violating Jewish law . . . According to your gospel Jesus died on the eve of Sabbath, a Jewish holy day – they are unlikely to perform or attend executions on Sabbath . . . St John also says that he died on the 14th of Nisan as though he were the Pascal lamb . . . there could be no execution on a Passover! – such a thing would be abhorrent. The crucifixion was an act of the Roman government who had persistently nailed Jews suspected of messianic ambitions to a cross – but, as I say, I cannot defend hypothetical crimes except by evidence of custom and law . . . in the same way Hugh's blood could never be used by us, but what hope for evidence – law – our religious discipline – you are determined to find us guilty!

First Prosecutor (*shouting*) This is heresy!

Judge (*coldly*) Continue, Rabbi.

Rabbi Ben Barachyal Our law repeatedly forbids human sacrifice and yet we are accused of repeatedly transgressing our law which is so sacred to us that many of us have chosen the stake and flames to baptism . . . of drinking blood which surely is a Christian custom celebrated in the Eucharist.

First Prosecutor (*shouting*) Must we be subjected to this abominable heresy in a Christian court?

Judge Do you expect this argument will endear a jury to mercy?

Monk (*aside to Rabbi*) Do you wish to carry on?

Rabbi Ben Barachyal (*to Monk*) I can do nothing else now . . . You accuse us of drinking blood and yet every time you celebrate Mass you devour the body of Jesus, his flesh and his blood – You take our metaphors and translate them literally – you really believe that your Lord's blood is in the wine truly, not symbolically, but *truly*, therefore *you* frequently drink blood – so of what are we accused? At the Last Supper a Rabbi celebrating his tribe's redemption at the hand of the Egyptians with the Passover wine and wafer, would not so transgress the law . . . 'Eating a man's flesh' is commonly used as a biblical metaphor meaning, to treat him with cruelty . . . as you have deigned to treat us, as your King has treated us, and your Popes – and for what reasons? (*trembling with rage and completely unconcerned now about saving their lives*) To unite your dividing ranks – to give them some common goal which is certain, which is real, nay, which is warm, which can be attacked, killed, vilified, to bleed us for your wars, for a scapegoat!

> *At this moment there is a huge uproar – the prosecution and jury has risen and are shouting over his voice as he carries on. Monk is visibly upset, Rabbi in state of collapse. His outburst was stimulated by a sense of futility, of being trapped. Some of the Knights have gone over and attacked the Monk and Rabbi, others trying to break them up.*

SCENE TWENTY-FIVE

A Voice The remaining seventy-four Jews in the Tower were released after two months, partly due to the continuous pleading on their behalf of the Franciscans, and an enormous fine. Eight years later, in 1263, the Barons attack Henry at Gloucester and he is defeated by Simon de Montfort . . . 1278, Edward, Henry's son, arrests the entire Jewish population on Friday 17th of November on a charge of counterfeiting coins . . . several hundred Jews were hanged . . . 1279, many London Jews torn asunder by horses on a charge of crucifying a child at Northampton . . . 1287, entire Jewish population again imprisoned – released under considerable ransom . . . 1290, Edward expels every Jew from English soil and confiscates all their property – some 16,500 Jews left a country they had lived in for over 400 years. Edmund, Luke's son, is now fifty-five and is troubled with bad dreams.

SCENE TWENTY-SIX

Edmund walks into the confession box at Lincoln Cathedral.

Edmund (*speaks to the priest, Arnold, who is now an old man*) Pray Father bless me, for I have sinned.

Arnold The Lord be in thy heart and on thy lips that thou mayest truly and humbly confess thy sins in the name of the Father, and of the Son and of the Holy Ghost.

Edmund I have sinned terribly Father.

Arnold Prostrate yourself humbly in the sight of God and pray Blessed Mary with the Holy Apostles and Martyrs to pray to the Lord for you – How have you sinned terribly?

Edmund (*in great difficulties*) I have horrible dreams that rack me.

Arnold Are they sinful dreams of illicit pleasure?

Edmund No – it is about my little brother Hugh.

Arnold He is resting peacefully, after all this time, you must feel no further guilt – he is our honoured Saint.

Edmund I see him in my dreams walking towards me with his hands dripping with blood, and he points his finger at me – and behind him are all the Jews coming towards me with knives . . .

Arnold How long have you had this dream?

Edmund Often – on and off for years!

Arnold God have mercy on you – why did you not come to me before?

Edmund I had to wait.

Arnold Why?

Edmund My father and mother – you see, I had to wait until they were dead before I could say anything.

Arnold Carry on, my son.

Edmund Because . . . little Hugh wasn't killed by the Jews.

Arnold You are disturbed, you don't know what you are saying.

Edmund I can't keep it inside me any more – it's eating me away and I thought if I told you, the dream would leave me – oh, I can't take the fear any more Father.

Arnold There is nothing to fear – you mustn't speak like this.

Edmund Please Father – let me confess – I lied about Hugh and the well, because I was afraid . . . He fell in it you see and I made up the story about him being chased because I thought they would beat me . . . but I didn't expect all that to happen – all that killing, and I couldn't speak until now – but it's been roaring inside me like a fire, destroying me . . . Oh Father! I've waited so many years to tell you this – so many years I've suffered this guilt – I've got blood on my hands – that's why my soul's tormented.

Arnold Have you confessed this to anyone else?

Edmund No Father.

Arnold Nor breathed a word?

Edmund No Father, I couldn't!

Arnold Your brother was canonised and the blessing of Sainthood conferred upon him – pilgrims come here from all over the land and miracles have taken place by his shrine – could we now un-Saint him – could we now explain the miracles that have happened?

Edmund (*upset*) I don't know Father.

Arnold You must say nothing more of this – it is as the Lord wished. Perhaps Hugh's death was meant to teach us something and to prevent an even greater tragedy – no Jew now rests on English soil – you unconsciously obeyed the will of God.

Edmund Will the dream stop coming then?

Arnold Of course it will stop – I absolve thee from thy sins . . . (*etc.*)

Edmund walks away from the cathedral which dissolves behind him. He walks for a few steps then stands and reflects upon the priest's words – he stands there quite still for a moment – then he lays down as if to sleep. After a moment he screams out in his sleep – he stands upright trembling. After a moment's consideration he stands up, takes off his belt which he ties into a noose and, attaching one end to a hook or to a wall, hangs himself.
The End.

MESSIAH

Scenes from a Crucifixion

Introduction

I began writing *Messiah* with the desire in mind to describe what a human being must have suffered on the cross, from their point of view so to speak. I saw this as a beginning rather than an end, since this is the image foremost in mind. I was not attempting to create an alternative point of view based on research, new theories or recent discoveries. Mine was an attempt to tell the story based on my own reactions to the Gospels and to foresee its links to the future.

However, during the time of writing I came across *The Passover Plot*, a remarkable book by Dr Hugh Schonfield (who was nominated for the Nobel Peace Prize in 1959) which fitted in with some of my own attitudes towards Jesus. Schonfield viewed the myth as more human than Godlike and evolved a remarkable theory based on much research and painstaking detail; the plot was in fact concocted by Jesus himself who engineers his own martyrdom since he sought to redeem the Jews and felt he could only do this through Messianic intervention. The Messiah had been expected eagerly for many years and now more than ever when Judah was under the yoke of Roman oppression.

The prophecies had been read carefully, if not with a certain desperation, and of course selectively to fit in with Messianic hope. Everybody reads what they wish to in any situation and the more stressful the situation the more apposite seems the philosophy that fits. Fortune-tellers are so successful in that the listener will eagerly bend any situation to 'fit' their own troubled souls. Schonfield's book is extraordinary on many levels and one feels one is reading scripture under a sharp white light.

I have woven this theory into *Messiah* as I too saw Jesus as more man than deity and thought it quite credible that he should wish to be the Messiah in order to bring about the new age. Like any young, idealistic and socially thinking man or woman today who wishes to change things and seeks the machinery of politics to achieve this, Jesus sought Messianic authority and the only way to accomplish this was to fulfil the prophets to the letter. Paradoxically we are taught to interpret Jesus through his parables and that he often used parables in order to deceive his simple Roman spies who would be paying close attention to what he was saying . . . Yet at the same time we are expected to interpret the Old Testament prophets *literally* to fit historical events!

Of course I used the Gospels for many of the speeches of Jesus and was able to see during rehearsals how much power they had to move one. They are inspiring and led me to believe that these may have been taken down verbatim by his disciples who would have followed him from one destination to another. The 'Sermon on the Mount' might well have been something he preached over and over again since he could only reach so many people at a time and why should he jettison so valuable a sermon merely to have a change of speech for each new setting? When his text was 'acted out', the reading became almost a litmus test for what might have been his authentic words. I have attempted to create his text and blend it in. Obviously I have taken some theatrical liberties with time and the locale. Most of all with the character of Satan who runs a gamut through history and becomes a mirror for all time and society from then until today. He reflects what he sees and if he sees the work of Satan dominant in our society rather than of God then that is how it is.

Characters

Jesus
John the Baptist
Mary
Satan
Pilate
Disciples
Judas
Soldiers
Priests
Caiphas
Scribe
Roman
Pharisees
Woman
Man
Chorus

During the month of March in the year 2000 we rehearsed the play for the first time in a workshop situation and performed it for a limited audience.

Messiah was first performed at Three Mills Studios, London, in March 2000.

The cast was as follows:

Jesus Rory Edwards
Mary / Woman Adjoa Andoh
John the Baptist Tim Walker
Satan Greg Hicks
Judas / Priest / Soldier 8 Ben Walden
Pilate / Soldier / Disciple / Priest 6 Gary Sefton
Caiphas / Scribe / Roman Raymond Sawyer

Soldiers / Priests / Chorus
Disciple 1 / Son Roddy McDevitt
Disciple 2 / Pharisee 2 David Kennedy
Disciple 3 Jan Knightley
Disciple 4 / Man Paul Sirr
Disciple 5 Malcolm James
Disciple 7 / Pharisee 1 Nigel Miles-Thomas

Director Steven Berkoff
Musician Mark Glentworth

Act One

SCENE ONE

Christ on the cross. Before him a group of soldiers playing dice.

Soldier 1 Throw the fuckin' dice . . .

Jesus My God, why hast Thou forsaken me / it hurts / Oh it hurts me / My swollen hands / my numb feet / as lumps of butcher's flesh / my raw and gaping side drips blood / Flies feed on me / First comes water / then blood / my life oozes out / Slowly / my mouth stinks / my breath harsh as sewers /

Soldier 1 Throw the fuckin' dice!

Soldier 2 OK, OK, keep your shirt on, just 'cause you're losin', don't get in a tantrum.

Soldier 3 I wish the bastard would fuckin' die and we could piss off.

Soldier 4 He'll die soon enough, poor sod.

Soldier 2 Double six, nice one!

Soldier 5 Jammy bugger! I'll have you for that.

Soldier 2 Go on then.

Jesus How long will it be? / I see the sun fastening its eye on me / I cling to the eye of God and feel calm / watch it slowly sink into the earth / I am drawn to it / its heat caresses and soothes me / the gentle wind cools my burning pain / My fingers swell up / my hands which were once so soft / hands that caressed and touched / cracked / splintered / Oh shame / it hurts /

Soldier 1 What ya staring at him for?

Soldier 2 He's distracting me from my game . . .

Soldier 3 Then ignore the git, ain't you seen enough crucifixions?

Jesus I don't want to feel pain / When they nailed my palms to the wood my eyeballs leapt / into my brain / could it be like this? / Fear squeezed my bowels and slimed the cross / They threw water and cleansed me / Don't look at me / mother don't see me / her hands cradling her face / her red raw eyes / She looks and looks away and looks again / don't / She is weeping for me / I hear her weeping.

Soldier 3 Nice one.

Soldier 8 Lovely.

Soldier 1 Give us a fag.

Soldier 3 I'm nearly skint.

Soldier 6 I'm having a piss. *turn around*

Jesus My mother who gave me life cries on her words / my father's hands support her / The soldiers hang around / They sit and play dumb games / and scratch and look at me / squinting their eyes against the sun / They wait for me to die.

Soldier 4 Not dead yet!

Soldier 5 Five hours and not dead yet.

Soldier 3 Die you bastard.

Soldier 1 We want to go home.

Soldier 2 Die you dog / You want another spear in your gut / eh?

Soldier 4 Then get on with it.

Soldier 7 Leave him be / He's OK.

Soldier 3 Your turn.

Soldier 4 Throw the fucking dice and stop staring at him.

Jesus Oow it hurts / it hurts / Help me / Where is he whose head speaks out for me above the throng of hypocrites / Who comforts me now as I drown in my own blood / and my heart splits and my tongue swells like an adder and cleaves to the roof of my mouth / my body drags the nails deeper into me as its pain yearns for the earth / my bloody vomit drips over my dry cracked lips /

Soldier 6 I must say he had a lot of bottle, I mean it took some fucking guts.

Soldier 8 What guts, the man's a fucking nutter.

Soldier 2 Going in there and smashing up the money changers.

Soldier 3 I mean you're asking for fucking trouble . . .

Soldier 7 He still had a lot of nerve, I mean knowing he's gonna get topped.

Soldier 8 Well, he didn't do it alone did he?

Soldier 3 It was a riot, fucking highly organised.

Soldier 5 To take over the fucking temple . . .

Soldier 2 He's a nutter.

Jesus Are you afraid of them? / Can you be afraid of bloated rats?

Soldier 6 Is he dead yet?

Soldier 8 Hey! (*shouting up*) You dead or what? Hahahaha!

Soldier 3 Throw the fuckin' dice . . .

Jesus The House of David will smite them that strike it / it shall arise like a blazing meteor / It is the star of life / It burns into my soul / It is the key to my father's house / Yea, on the door of my father's house it blazes forth / It confuses them that create disorder / for it is order / It will confuse the cruel and the ignorant will smash it / its enemies will have signs that are jagged and vicious / The symbols of their houses will be swords / daggers and skulls / They will worship death and not the mysteries of life / They will bless themselves with their signs and think themselves holy while nailing up more men /

Soldier 2 Die you dog and shut up.

Soldier 3 If you're so clever / If you're the King of the Jews . . .

Soldier 4 Come off the cross / Ha ha.

Soldier 5 That's a good one.

Soldier 3 I'll take odds on that.

Soldier 8 Let him rant on / Your throw.

Jesus They will kill me again and yet again / while blaming others / they will kill the son and say the father did it / They will kill and kill / and murder in my name / In my name Oh my God they will murder / not in their own /

Soldier 1 Shut it!

Soldier 2 So he's a fuckin' commie, yeah, wants to take over the fucking world . . .

Soldier 3 Listen I hate them, I really fuckin' hate 'em.

Soldier 4 'Cause they want what you and I have sweated for . . .

Soldier 1 What you got you cunt? You ain't got two pence to scratch your arse with . . .

Soldier 4 I work for what I've got, right . . .

Soldier 1 He wants the poor to rise against the rich, yeah, 'cause they're lazy bastards!

Soldier 3 I mean that's his fucking message, that's why everyone's for him.

Soldier 6 So you start with the temple, right, grab hold of that and you're halfway there . . .

Soldier 8 You sound like you approve of the bastard! You should watch yourself.

Soldier 3 Throw it!

Jesus It is nearly over / my body comes alive again / it's not been alive / it pours out of me / I dissolve into light / I stream forth / I am on fire / I am hung on threads of gold / My heart feels rich / the last drops of blood soak the earth / I fly out in a divine line that is perfect / My dry and dead body I bequeath to earth / My spirit floats in the air / I see myself below / a piece of decay and stink / above / I fly to the sun / I float up above the crowd / drawn up like moisture into the body of Him.

Soldier 3 Who farted?

Jesus Oh father / Oh mother / do not weep and heave yourselves into each other's breast / Look up / Look up / See me / see me as a shadow in front of the sun / See me arise / Look up / Look up / Yes, that's good / You see me in your dreams and smile / I become joy / I become light / I am alive . . .

Soldier 3 Double six.

Soldier 2 Nice one.

Soldier 3 Did ya think he's the King of the Jews?

Soldier 4 Don't make me laugh! He's the gang leader of a bunch of fuckin' weirdos, bandits, that's all.

Soldier 5 There's a thousand of 'em hanging along the highway . . .

Music.

SCENE TWO

Pilate What can I do? / I washed my hands of the whole affair / I did it in public / They want him nailed to the post / So be it / and on the eve of Passover / Now Barrabas was offered . . .

Scribe And they refused. My Lord Pilate, they wish to take him down.

Pilate Who?

Scribe The Jew they call Jesus before the Sabbath comes in. That's the law. Their law forbids a dead man polluting the Sabbath.

Pilate Is he dead yet?

Scribe Very close.

Pilate Then let him hang around a little longer . . .

Scribe But there might be a riot!

Pilate But I washed my hands in public / That means I have no blood of his on me / That's good, people love gestures.

Scribe That's why they flock to the theatre.

Pilate I couldn't care less / let them have him / But let us consider / Who is 'them'? / The mob / You think I listen to the mob / but you will write that the crowd shouted ...

Scribe Crucify him!

Chorus No!

Pilate Did not one voice struggle to be heard / Not one voice to shout ... Save him!

Scribe No, I heard nothing.

Pilate From all the thousands that hung on him / with all his miracles did not one show up except his enemies / But scripture will say the crowd shouted ...

Chorus Crucify him!

Pilate Crucify him! And who am I to dispute scripture / It must be written that the crowd shouted together as one man / and then I said / I am not responsible for his death / This is your doing / your doing / the mob! / Shall I be an executioner for a dirty mob / I, Pilate the Great / But scripture will say ...

Chorus Let the punishment for his death fall upon us Hebrews and upon our children ...

Pilate Ah! Very clever that! I am absolved by scripture for ever / They condemned their innocent and yet unconceived and unborn children / and their unborn and on and on for ever more / and who? All the crowd / Some of the crowd / A crowd in the square condemns the unborn millions / Could they represent them? / But scripture will say ...

Chorus On our children.

Pilate On their children ... And who am I to dispute it / and when the descendants of Abraham will be destroyed we cannot interfere for so it is written / I can find no reason for his death / Write that down as well / I had him flogged OK? / Shall I let him go? / Go on / let him off the hook?

Chorus Nooo! Break his legs.

Pilate To break his legs. You're fastidious aren't you? No, you can't. Let him stay there and enjoy the sun a little longer. Are you the King of the Jews? I asked him / Go on answer me.

Jesus These are your words.

Pilate Well of course they're my bloody words you filthy Hebrew swine / You want another taste of it / Have you written that down? / I can find no reason for his death / Look at him / Of course I can find a thousand reasons / His very existence threatens all we have / Every breath he takes sucks the breath out of me / He's inspiring / When you hear him speak / He enchants the air / The mob eats out of his hands / He would unite them against us / They would die like flies for the touch of him / My power would fly out of the window / He could unmake us all / Too much belief / far too much / Look at him / It was your people that handed you over you know / He doesn't believe a word / Of course not / Look at his face / The mob would become an almighty fist and break us / so you have to be destroyed / But don't set that down you fool / set down that I can find no crime against him / Set it down that I offered him to the people as a Passover gift.

Scribe That's beautiful.

Pilate And they repeated . . .

Scribe Let his death be a punishment upon us / for ever.

Pilate Very nice . . . Future crimes against them will no longer be crimes but just deserts.

Scribe Good.

Pilate God-killers!

Scribe That's right!

Pilate Yes, and kill those two bastards with him.

Scribe Oh very good. Dangerous zealots!

Pilate Call them bandits / don't call them zealots! /
Whatever you do don't use that word / Yes he was
crucified with two bandits / I was curious / I have to
admit that when I saw him / this slim and fine young
man / Such eyes that could pierce into your innermost
secrets / I could barely look at him / He has a way of
making those with secrets feel guilty but beautiful my
God how beautiful he is / Is still, even hanging there /
A body like a woman so soft and hair so fine / Not
typical of them / not frizzy but delicate / Like a woman's
hair / and lips so taut / Long / wide mouth / beautiful
raging pucking strident mouth / beautiful mouth / My
God he was a lovely creature / What a waste / My wife
had a dream about him after she saw him / She had a
very bad dream / it disturbed her / I think she dreamed
he was stirring up that crock of decayed hope / She
dreamed he came into her chamber / entered her bed
and ravished her / There I've said it / Don't put that in
you dog / She dreamed that . . . She said she had a bad
dream and suffered on his account. Put that down /
I find nothing that he has said offensive, I can find no
charges against him / Put that down, just put that down
I say / I don't want them to come against us in years to
come / We must be spotless / Say, I am not responsible
for this man's death / this is your doing. Never mind
about the five thousand / No one spoke for him in the
crowd / Never mind you heard the wailing of a river /
the crashing of a storm saying . . .

Chorus Free him.

Pilate In rhyme to Jesus / Never mind a thousand voices rose like the breaking of a dam and shook the lintel of the window / and even cracked the windows / in one huge howl / Never mind that a thousand centurions were needed to hold back the crowd / whose combined voice as thunder shouted . . .

Chorus Save him.

Pilate Never mind and never mind and never mind / They said 'Crucify him' / Put that down!

Scribe Shall we put down that he was betrayed by his own people . . . One of his own disciples betrayed him?

Pilate Very good. Set that down too. What was his name?

Scribe Judas.

Pilate Very good. The name fits. JU–DAS!

Chorus Judas, betrayed him, Judas . . .

SCENE THREE

Judas Stink and slime / Alone I am in a haze of stink / that with a kiss / I betrayed my master / A kiss of silver / thirty pieces / No don't use that expensive perfumed oil on him /

Priests Stink.

Jesus I thirst.

Judas 'Leave her be,' he said / 'It's all she has / How long will I be here / She anoints me for my end.' 'We could sell it for the poor,' I said.

Jesus I'm burning.

Judas 'The poor will always be with us,' he shouted at me / 'I will be gone / Leave her.' I said, 'Don't talk to me like that! / Not in front of the others.' / He sits and she moulds his soft skin with her perfumed fingers / very nice! / How much / twenty? Make it thirty.

Priests That's too much!

Jesus I hunger.

Judas That's my lowest.

Priests Meet us halfway / twenty-five?

Judas No! Thirty, take it or leave it!

Priests You're a hard man / Times is hard in the trade / We are not dripping exactly with wealth.

Judas Thirty!

Priests Give him the thirty pieces of silver!

Judas He doesn't care / To tell the truth I am doing him a favour.

Jesus I'm afraid.

Judas Without me there's no show / Without me the prophecies can't come true / He needs help / He needs me / He *needs* me / He wants it / the nailing / It has to be / nails piercing through sinew and splintering the bone / The blood spitting out in waves from the ruptured pipes / A great crimson spray / the swollen ankles turning blue / The look of it / He's always if you like, been attracted to it / Arms akimbo, head lolling / eyes rolling to heaven / Very inspirational for artists / Fulfilling scripture we are not, unless I do it / but I am still covered in stink / I was the cover-up / thirty pieces / No I am not coming down / that's the price / He begged me / Do it for me Judas / not in so many words / but in prophecies / indications / He loved the cross / always talked about the time when he would be there / His eyes would glaze / Aren't you afraid?

Jesus It hurts.

Judas Why? he answered. My father would send me down twelve armies of angels to defend me if I wish / but then the scriptures wouldn't come true / I am he, the Messiah / Twelve armies of angels / what a beautiful sight that would be.

Priests Stink.

Judas He wanted to go while he was still beautiful and still covered in that sweet smell / and I'm covered in . . .

Priests Stink.

Judas For being the straight man / Me!

Jesus I thirst.

Judas He looked at me and begged me with his eyes / but how could I betray him / I loved him! / But he looked at me / that was enough / He put his hand in the dish and gave it to me.

Jesus I ache.

Judas I said the man whom I kiss is yours / They didn't need me / They didn't need me / They had seen him a hundred times! / They had seen him in front of thousands! / They *knew* him / I needed to point him out!? / The guy was famous / I did nothing for my money except take it.

Priests Stink.

Judas I hate the money / Take it back.

Priests We don't want it / Take it / It's yours. You earned it.

Judas I throw it in your faces / Blood money.

Priests Use it for a graveyard.

Jesus I weep.

Judas I did what I had to do and now he's on the beloved cross / and I am festering alone covered in stink which will be my everlasting scent / It penetrates to the marrow of my bones and for all time / He radiates while I become the expedient worm on the end of his hook / He luminesces and beams / His thorny perch becomes him.

Jesus I'm burning.

Judas He illuminates in the sun / I stink / The smell is getting worse / I think I'll go hang myself.

Priests Yeah that's a good idea / Where's a stout piece of hemp?

Judas I will smell worse and foul up the tree / but I won't be here / I will bloat like a balloon and burst / It's the only way to get rid of the stench / that I acquired for him / I hope it did some good / He's all right / You Jesus.

Jesus I become light, I become joy, I am alive.

Disciples take Jesus off cross – carry him to Mary.

SCENE FOUR

Mary (*mourning, her son is in her arms*) He was my son from out of my loins, from out of my stomach came forth he in a sack of blood / He grew in my womb, he swelled me and out of my thighs he slid in a mess of warm afterbirth / But he didn't look like Joseph, he looked like God / God came to me in a dream and made love to me and in the morning I knew I had been visited by a god / In a dream he came and slid between Joseph and me / and as Joseph tried to enter me, God slipped into his place / He was beautiful and strong and said 'Mary I have come for you / I want to enter you and pour my spirit into you and make your body a cave for my child, and this child will be my son / He is the son of man, he'll be everything perfect / Everything that humans try to be he will be' / Why me? 'Why not you?' he said. He came to earth to my small bed of straw and held me tight and poured his seed into me and he was glowing as if on fire and touched Joseph to keep him sleeping and God filled me up with love and when you make love God is there with his angels and they, the angels, worked deep in my womb / I felt them fluttering within making the sinews and small veins and weaving tissues and arranging the nerves and putting everything in perfect order and pasting on the delicate limbs and rounding the sockets and moulding the perfect shape of his eyes and then painting the colour of the eyes and whispering into his new brain the secrets of the universe and telling him who he is so he should know / and all through the night they worked on the act of creation and on a tiny fingernail of a tiny angel was the pulse to start the engine of life / and the angel carried it to this small soft thing and sewed it into him and then bound him to me to nourish and to feed / and when the work was done God opened his hand and they flew into his hand like a swarm of bees to the hive and he clasped them all gently, one million of them and dissolved into a beam of early morning sunlight and melted away . . . He was meek, He was mild, He was gentle, He was our son.

SCENE FIVE

Jesus gets up slowly. Disciples bring him clothes, shoes.
He dresses as he speaks.

Jesus I came to set the earth on fire! Do you suppose
I came to bring peace to the world? Not peace but
conflict! Father against son, son against father, mother
against daughter, daughter against mother / Do you
think that I came to bring peace to the world / No I did
not come to bring peace but a sword, a man's worst
enemy will be his own family / not true? No prophet is
recognised in his own country. How blessed are you who
are hungry / Your hunger will be satisfied.

Judas We hear you.

Jesus How blessed are you who weep now, you shall
laugh / How blessed are you when men hate and insult
you, and ban your name as infamous, on that day be
glad and dance for joy.

Disciple 6 Amen.

Jesus But alas you who are rich, you have had your time
of happiness. Alas for you who are well fed now, you
shall go hungry / Alas for you who laugh now, you shall
mourn and weep.

Disciple 7 We hear you.

Jesus If your right eye is your undoing then pluck it out /
It is better for you to lose one part of your body than for
the whole of it to be flung into hell.

Disciple 1 Amen.

Jesus And if your right hand is your undoing, cut it off
and fling it away.

Disciple 2 Amen.

Jesus If someone slaps you on the right cheek, offer him your left / If he wants your shirt, give him your coat as well / You have learned, love your neighbour, hate your enemy, but I tell you love your enemies and pray for them.

Disciples 3 and 5 Hallelujah!

Jesus If you only pray for those that love you what reward can you expect.

Disciples 4 and 6 Right!

Jesus Even tax collectors do that. In your prayers do not babble like the heathen who imagine the more they say the more they are likely to be heard, do not imitate them.

Disciples 1 and 2 Never!

Jesus Don't be like the hypocrites / No servant can be a slave of two masters, for he will hate the first and love the second.

Disciples 2 and 5 We hear you!

Jesus You cannot serve God and money / Put away anxious thoughts about clothes and money to keep you alive / Surely life is more to you than food and clothes / Look at the birds of the air.

Disciple 5 Tell us.

Jesus They do not store in barns, yet your heavenly father feeds them / Are you not worth more than the birds? / Why be anxious about clothes / consider how the lilies grow in the fields, they do not work or spin and yet Solomon in all his glory was not attired like one of these.

Disciple 1 Yeah! That's the truth!

Jesus Do not moan anxiously about what shall we eat, we drink, what shall we wear.

Disciples 4 and 7 No, no!

Jesus The heathen chases these, not you, your heavenly father knows that you need them. Pass no judgement so you shall not be judged.

Judas Tell us.

Jesus Do not look at the speck in your brother's eye and ignore the plank in your own. Hypocrite!

Disciples 1 and 2 More, more!

Jesus Clean your own eyes first then you'll see clearly the speck in your brother's / Do not throw your pearls before swine / they will trample them to pieces. Enter by the narrow gate. The gate that is wide leads to perdition. Beware of false prophets. You will recognise them by the fruit they bear.

Disciple 5 Tell us.

Jesus Can grapes be picked on briars or figs on thistles? A good tree yields good fruit and a poor tree bad fruit, and when a tree does not yield good fruit it is cut down and burnt.

Disciples 3 and 6 That's right.

Jesus The man who acts on my words builds his house on a rock, neither rain nor storm will budge it, but a man who hears and does not act on them builds his house on sand.

Disciple 1 He does.

Disciple 2 Yes.

Disciple 1 More, more.

Jesus The rains came down, the floods rose and down it fell with a great crash.

Roar of the crowd / Ecstasy / Hallelujah! Amen!

SCENE SIX

Jesus and Disciples.

Jesus How did it go tonight?

Disciple 5 You were great / really.

Disciple 3 Great / terrific.

Disciple 4 Straight up.

Disciple 2 It was a knockout smash, J.C.

Jesus I didn't overdo it?

Disciple 2 Nah? Listen to 'em, they're still sitting around like for the other shows they can't wait to get out but with you boss / you can't give them enough.

Disciple 5 There's a few lepers backstage to see you.

Jesus Oh God, not more lepers! Any ladies around?

Disciple 2 Yeah, we got a couple lined up.

Jesus Nice?

Disciple 2 Sweet as persimmons.

Jesus Very nice.

Disciple 1 There were a few Romans snooping around, sniffing here and there / grabbing an earful.

Jesus That's good.

Disciple 6 They looked worried / like you were pulling a big mob out there / worried like you might turn a head or two.

Jesus Ain't that the plan?

Disciple 5 Go easy J.C.

Disciple 7 Step at a time.

Disciple 2 They've too much muscle.

Jesus For now / It won't be long.

Disciple 3 Don't spoil the plan.

Jesus We'll take over the world.

Disciple 5 Step at a time.

Jesus First Jerusalem.

Disciple 1 We'll get there / in time.

Jesus Time is running out.

Disciple 3 Keep in with them / for now.

Judas Your mother's calling for you.

Jesus I have no mother / my family are here.

Judas Your soup's on the table.

Jesus Someone will eat it!

Disciple 3 Pilate is scratching his bald head when he thinks of you / You've put ants in his ears.

Jesus Let it gnaw his brain.

Disciple 3 The ants will starve on that diet! Step at a time.

Disciple 5 Look what they did to John.

Disciple 7 The truth burned them.

Jesus His words flayed them alive.

Judas Yeah, but he lost his head in the excitement.

Disciple 3 Someone wants to touch your cloak.

Jesus OK. Get it over with.

Disciple 3 Finished.

Disciple 6 Too bad about John.

Disciple 7 He was a character. He wore some very strange clobber.

Disciple 2 Some punters were nervous to go near him.

Jesus What do you mean?

Disciple 1 Like what he wore.

Judas It put people off.

Disciple 4 Like he was a freak.

Jesus Who cares what you wear on your skin. It's what you carry in your heart. You think God says you can't come in without a jacket. You think heaven's a five-star restaurant for the rich – Tip the head waiter for a good seat – God's temple can be in a river. His spirit is in the water of that stream. In a barn was I born, in the stink of cow-dung and that smelled to me sweeter than the perfumes of the harlots who sit in the gallery of the temple while their husbands sit below whispering share prices.

Disciple 3 That sounds like your next sermon, Jesus, Holy Rabbi, Master and Superjew?

Jesus It is my sons, my devoted disciples / It's for the money changers who shall donate to our cause.

Disciple 5 I think you've whipped them enough, J.C.

Jesus Next time they'll pay or they'll get more of the same.

Disciple 4 They have to earn a crust.

Jesus Then let them throw a few crusts to those without. Get on to that Judas / fund-raiser and keeper of the purse. But who comes here? A Roman centurion.

Disciple 2 Oi! Gavalt!

Jesus Don't shit a brick you men of little faith / He looks troubled / Say what your business is / you emissary from the nether world / Heathen / Unbeliever / Pilate's muscle / Bully boy of the state / Idol licker / Oppressor and bacon nosher.

Roman Lord, my servant lies paralysed / you can heal him / I am not worthy to have you come under my roof but say the word and I know he will be healed.

Jesus Well that saves me a shlep! Now there's a man with a lot of faith / and never in Israel have I found such faith. I tell you he'll sit at the table in heaven while many of you will sit out in the cold. Go, centurion, and consider it done.

Disciple 6 Nice one Jesus.

Disciple 4 An ally in the other camp.

Judas We'll cash that cheque some day.

Jesus Be wise as serpents and innocent as doves. Remember what happened to John / Do not fear those who kill the body but cannot kill the soul.

Man Master . . . I brought my son to you. He's possessed / He falls to the ground / He's speechless / He foams at the mouth / Goes rigid.

Jesus Apart from that is he all right?

Man Oh yes, it's only that. I asked your disciples to cast it out. But it's so strong they couldn't.

Jesus You unbelieving and perverse generation / How long must I endure you? / You couldn't even do this / What are ye? / You bunch of simpering failures / Is it with ye I shall set the world on fire? / Could you not even trap the devil in him and cast him out? / Is all my training wasted? Faith is what you need. Faith. You have faith the size of a mustard seed . . . You need faith that can move mountains / You can stop the earth with faith / Nothing will be impossible for you with faith.

Disciple 3 (*aside*) The crowd's building up.

Jesus Deaf and dumb spirit. I command that you come out of him and never go back.

Son Jesus Christ.

Judas If only John could see you now, Jesus.

SCENE SEVEN

John the Baptist – the Head.

John the Baptist I see him / I see him / even if my head is on a plate / my soul is in the sky / my words stung like hornets until their black hearts were festered in boils / They cut off my head / but my words ring in the air / they hang in the air as echoes that will never fade / I was washed clean in the waters of the Jordan / I baptised him / He came to me / and I held him under the swirling waters / then pulled him up / the river dancing through his hair and branching over his face like a thousand diamonds glittering in the sun / and he laughed and I laughed and he held onto me and the waters rose round us / and I said I need to be baptised by you / and you come to me / and he said / I want you to do it for me / I want your hands holding me under / I want the waters pouring over me / Oh sweet waters / Long have I walked to witness thee / to hear thy sounds rage over the lands / but beware / they will snare you / They put me in dungeons / and cut off my head but still it talks on / no

one can stop it / Even in my stinking dungeon pit I smelt
their rottenness which penetrated my walls / even under
the perfumes I smelt decay / Their flesh was rotten, fruit
that was loose and fleshy / it might come away in your
hands / The decay of wealth / of a spirit withered by
indolence / and rum babas / Through lack of purpose
the fibre and coil of muscle and skin was as overcooked
meat / Their mouths were petulant and saggy as those of
the daughters of merchants that hang loose in disappointed
desire / never straightened by determination / their eyes
were as yellow amber from the poisons of their plate /
and their teeth were as crumbling chalk from lack of
struggle / They stuffed into their gobbling mouths sweet
and evil / the brains of sheep / the balls of calves / the
slime in the shells of fish / the marrow of bones / the
soft jelly of the eye / the frail texture of the lung / Never
what is hard and fresh / but slugs / worms / snakes /
drank from the blood of beasts / sucked from the teats of
asses / and then not satisfied they desired on a plate my
head / my head on a plate and so it was / I was put on a
silver dish which caught my hot blood still oozing from
my freshly ripped veins / and as they looked from their
yellow indolent sickly eyes I opened my mouth / Yea
even from the plate I opened my mouth / Their souls
curdled and their eyes looked as if to crack / There on
the bloody plate, my blood still pulsing out / I opened
my bloody mouth and howled / I howled to heaven /
Then they hurled me to the floor where I lay / Some time
passed / my body was buried / by my disciples / my mind
lives on.

Jesus His mind will always live on / Spread the word /
The time is running out / Once for John and now for me /
I must do it as it is said it should be done / OK enough
of that / Bring in the ladies! Sweet as persimmons / There
is time for everything / and for everything there is time /

Woman / I want your tears shed for me / I want my feet
bathed in a lake of tears / I want the dirt of my feet
washed in the salty warm tears of loose women, then
after I want my dirt and your tears wiped away by your
hair your soft hair on my feet / your long soft hair
caressing my feet mixed with the moist thick drops of
your anguish and then please kiss my feet / I love your
lips on my gnarled feet / your tongue and lips kissing my
bruised feet and gently holding them. Then after she has
wept her silken tears on my feet and dried them with her
hair / After she has done this / give me some wine / After
this she may anoint my feet with myrrh and then slowly
and softly massage them and since such a great love is
shown . . . (to woman) I shall forgive you. I forgive you.
You are forgiven.

Judas But Jesus, she is only a whore.

Jesus I forgive her.

Disciple 6 She is a whore.

Jesus Your sins are forgiven.

Disciple 2 But she's a whore.

Jesus All your sins are forgiven by your great love.

Disciple 2 You forgive a whore?

Jesus You provided no water for my feet, she gave me
tears. You gave me no kiss but she kissed my feet. You
didn't anoint my head with oil, she anointed my feet
with myrrh. Feet . . . Feet . . . Feet . . . soon a nail will
go through these feet.

Act Two

SCENE ONE

Temptation.

Jesus I'm hungry / Twenty days I have fasted / I'm so hungry the stones look like bread, my stomach is glued to my spine / I thirst / I see visions / I am mad / Hunger can drive you mad / My mouth is dry leather ready to crack.

Satan Jesus, give it up / You can, you have the power / Twenty days and twenty to go / You are mad, turn the stones into bread / Do it / no one will know.

Jesus I will know / I will always know / Don't alter the shape of things / Stones are stones / If I give in now how will I endure what is to come / The stones look like loaves but they are stones / Don't alter God's design / My mouth aches / my stomach is a knot. I couldn't eat / I could drink / My lips are black / the sun burns, the wind cuts / the north wind that ripens and destroys.

Satan Turn the stones into bread / tasty crisp bread / Sabbath bread / soft, moist and sweet / milk bread holy bread soft and spongy / bread that breaks in your fingers / that pulls away in your fingers like a soft persimmon / Chew it soft and warm / smelling warm motherly warm / The stones are loaves / they smell good / just out of the oven and crisp / warm as newborn babes.

Jesus Man cannot live by bread alone.

Satan Oh very good / If you are who they say you are / and if you say you are who you think you are / throw yourself off this parapet and if you are the son of God

He will send down His angels to bear you up lest you strike yourself against the stones.

Jesus Do not put God to the test.

Satan I will give you everything if you kneel down to me.

Jesus I serve one God alone / only in Him do I believe so back, Satan / back to your leathery pit / back to your filthy cave / Snake, you tempt me not / you are too stupid you missed what I want / I came to set the world on fire / You offer me palaces – I will inherit the Kingdom of Heaven / I will ride on chariots of fire / I will sit on the right hand of Him who is greater than anything in the world.

SCENE TWO

The Devil.

Satan Now that was a waste of time / this man is a lost cause to me / In temptation / there is only one thing that tempts him / power / I was too late / for him anyway / What tempts you? What you fear to have tempts you / It's what you fear to possess but would like to possess that tempts you / What you crave in your heart of hearts / Some want gold dripping through their fingers while others want sperm / I can make you bastards lust like you have never known it / but you must be tempted / What can you be tempted by? / By what you haven't got / or think you shouldn't have or are too timid to demand / so Satan comes to help you / Satan is good to you / you cannot be tempted by what you loathe / can you? / Of course not / only by what you crave secretly in your private soul / you are afraid to do / you have been forbidden / frightened off / Priest fearing / God fucking /

knee bending / ass licking / I can give you what you
dream of but lack the hand or the will to do / I stiffen
your flaccid will / I put fire in your guts / I put blood in
you / I put steel in your flesh / conscience it is that robs
it / fear that shrivels its purpose / Call on me Oh Satan
for your best fucks / I will make you fuck like a poker /
I will drown your mind in visions manifold / I will release
you from the fear that binds you to be mere mortals and
make you giants / You will be a ram / you will be as a
devil / Temptation by Satan is only coming face to face
with yourself / Satan is the half of you that you hate /
or have been made to hate / Satan lurks in the corner
of your eye / when walking, your wife by your side /
a beautiful creature passes / I feel a tug on my sleeve /
Satan is called / I hear cries from all over the city / like a
great wail from the collected agony of frustration / of the
bored of the lonely stirring themselves with the thoughts
of Satan / How then is Satan bad? / Satan is not bad /
for he is the part of you that you have been made to
crush / So I lurk in your dreams / I swim in your daily
thoughts / You say one thing and mean another / Even
the priests call me / I hear thoughts calling on me / I put
strength in the murderer's hands / I put the spark in the
rapist's eye / I put ambitious greed in the politician /
I put desire in the thief / I put pictures in the mind of the
masturbator / I put even more greed in the rich / filthy
consuming greed / so they are never satisfied / I put
malice and viciousness in the poor / I inspire rulers to
make one law for them and one for the poor / Kings and
Queens will eat fortunes while the millions starve / This
is the rule of Satan / I can put doubt in the Christians /
I will confuse them / they will preach goodness with a
Bible in one hand while the other cuts their brothers'
throats / I shall put causes in the minds of the mad /
I will put jealousy in the innocent / lust in the mother /
But I only come when I am called / When I am needed /

I do not have to go out like the Christians and convert
the heathens and give them the pox / good Christian pus /
At the same time / I wait / I wait for the desire / I gave
them all the will / I allow the Satan side of man to
manifest itself / it is there dormant within / ready to step
out once it is fed the germ of want / God, your God says
deny all that / all that energy / that wealth of power /
You're right, I could not tempt him / I didn't expect to /
He has all he wants / He believes he is the son of God /
Self-deception is the great drug / I put desire in those
whose pleasure is others' pain / I put invention in the
torturer / I give inspiration to orgies / I bless those that
hurl themselves into a sea of flesh / In what is excessive
is where I lurk / I despise possessive love / the shrill
aching boredom of a priest-blessed union / the death-
knell of repetition / the aching desire like a great bird
locked in a filthy cage of self-doubt and fear / Your timid
morsels of Christian lust are as thin as your watery soup
and your uninspired table / The great fiery lusts of
women must be led by Satan / Satan is your real face
before your God buried it / Not the face of miserable
and insufferable goodness / thin-lipped self-denial /
weakness / Help old ladies across the street / live only in
fantasy while stirring that crock of decay that lies farting
next to you / Torture yourself with all the things that
you are denied / Don't look in hurt envy at the riches of
those who stamp all over you / you are made to be
stamped on / you are instructed to be a doormat for
them / If you don't like it worship me and be like them /
The jewels of the world are yours if you come to me /
I will be the mirror of your soul / deny me and you deny
yourself that you love / I am your sweet morsel of carnal
delight / I am the precious gleam in your gold / I am the
flesh that drools and hangs over your guts / I am the
saliva in your fat greedy mouths / the hump in your back
from counting your money is mine too / the spleen

arising from your throat too is mine / Deny me and you shrivel / Deny me and you fear / You fear to look around every corner / You fear the robber stealing your little hoard for he is armed by Satan / you are disarmed / you fear every knock on the door / you fear to open your mouth / Deny me and you are without / you are caught in obsessions / tossed this way and that / without a guide to lead you / You become a dog howling in the wind / neurosis is yours / obsession over nothing is yours / madness is yours / madness is denial of Satan / cast out in the void / thrown into the maelstrom / paralysed by doubt and fear / Shall I do this? / Shall I do that? / Where shall I go? / What shall I do? / Oh dear, help me / Death – death without me – Death / gnawing your bone of obsession / fighting off the reality inside you / You become trapped in your fears / You cannot move / you are sinking in your swamp of filthy self-doubt / you become ugly / you are afraid to show your face / you hide / you snivel / you make little weak sounds / you make squeaking noises of appeasement / instead of worshipping me your master / you tremble and lick ass / you lick your guvnor's ass because he is guided by me / that's why he rules you / you tremble without me / your wife will be frail like you, and you will live in drudgery / staring at the demands that come through the door as if they were some kind of holy text / With your wide watery eyes you will work for peanuts because God said so / You will honour authority because it is written in scripture / 'Every person must submit to the extreme authorities, discharge your obligation, pay tax and toil' / They use it on themselves / You will work until you die for them / and then a vulture in black will say mumbo over your grave / Even in death you will be made poorer / and while you lie there in shrill expectancy of angels and the great gates of heaven opening you suddenly find yourself with a mouthful of mud and dog turds / You

will lie there waiting for what you have been promised /
for what you denied yourself for all these years / lest you
spoilt your chances of getting there / Maybe it's tomorrow
you hope / maybe they're busy up there or short-staffed /
and slowly you will rot and stink and turn to ooze and
even then you will say, if you could say it, 'I've been
conned.'

SCENE THREE

The Conspiracy.

Jesus Away with you Satan / you think as men think /
not as God thinks / Never mind him / he comes at you
like a thief in the night / you see him sliding up in the
corner of your eye / like a rat / He never confronts you
face to face / he would shrivel at the impact / Only when
you stumble / you falter / you weaken / you doubt / Then
there he is / like a germ in your sickness / he is the
disease in your mind / On the Day of Judgement he will
be condemned by his own words.

Disciple 3 Master, we're hungry.

Disciple 4 Starving.

Disciple 5 I can eat a horse, I mean a cow.

Jesus Then pluck some ears of corn. Stroll through the
grain fields, it's a nice day.

Disciple 5 What's that hiding in the bushes?

Jesus Those are Pharisees.

Disciple 6 What are they doing here?

Jesus Checking up on us / to condemn us for working
on the Sabbath.

Disciple 4 Who put them there?

Jesus Spies.

Disciple 3 What for?

Jesus So I can say the Son of Man is Lord of the Sabbath and condemn a few more Pharisees.

Disciples Oh . . .

Disciple 5 It's a trap.

Pharisee 1 Excuse me, are they your mates?

Jesus Yes.

Pharisee 2 I suppose you know what time it is.

Jesus In God's world there is only one time and that is when you give yourself to him.

Pharisee 1 Never mind all that / You're in this bleedin' world now, mate / and tell your colleagues to stop nicking that grain on the Sabbath.

Jesus The Son of Man is Lord of the Sabbath / You serpents and vipers . . .

Pharisee 2 Don't you go using that language on us!

Jesus Is it sinful to save life on the Sabbath?

Pharisee 1 Look, I'm just the keeper here / just clear off out of it / or I'll report you to the authorities.

Jesus Go / You will flee from the wrath to come / You and all your kind will writhe in everlasting torment.

Pharisee 1 Get out of it / and tell your mates to get a bloody haircut / son of God!?

Pharisee 2 He wouldn't have any of you in the house . . .

Jesus Listen, I don't want you to tell people that I'm the Messiah.

Disciple 3 We won't utter a dickybird.

Jesus I've got to keep cool, see . . .

Disciple 5 We gotcha, keep a low profile and then spring it on 'em. We don't want to be stopped / early days, right?

Jesus Right! Listen pals, I have to go to Jerusalem tomorrow. I've gotta stir things up with the elders / First of all, the temple, that's the aim, stop them paying tribute to the Romans, so we disrupt the money changers, turn over a few stalls, disrupt the sacrifices . . .

Disciple 4 But they're only small fry, trying to earn a living, make a crust . . .

Judas Sell a few doves for the temple offerings . . .

Disciple 3 What will that do, Jeez?

Jesus Stop the money flow that's haemorrhaging out. The temple money is God's money, it comes from our blood and labour. Give me a coin – see this coin?

Disciples Yeah . . .

Jesus It's got Caesar's face on it right?

Disciples OK . . .

Jesus Then let him have it. But when you take it to the temple it gets changed into the special temple money . . .

Disciples Right . . .

Jesus And that money belongs to God, for the sacrifices, for the fabric of the temple, for the stones, the altar, the scrolls, the scribes. By giving a tribute of that money we defile the temple, we pollute it, raising money for God's work and giving it to heathens . . . Don't you see?

130

Judas Yeah, we've got you.

Jesus So we create a disturbance, no more temple money to the Romans . . .

Disciple 5 That's it! Get rid of the collaborators!

Jesus No doubt cause a few red ears among the Romans / They'll call me a revolutionary or zealot / others a blasphemer / I'll get topped in other words / the Big Cross / but I'll rise again in three days. That's the plan. Tell Ma to keep the soup on a small light. I'll be back to finish it.

Disciples Nice one, Manny.

Jesus Three days, that's all I need, to fulfil the prophecies of Isaiah / I've gotta do it. I've told you all this before and I'll tell you again / I'll be nailed down. Can I take it? We'll see, but if we don't do it we don't fulfil scriptures. And I must rise / three days that's all I need. Now you must take me down off the cross before sunset / that's the plan / OK.

Disciples Right!

Jesus I'll arrange the provocation / I'll blaspheme / I'll say I'm the son of God / contrary to the commandment / 'Thou shalt worship no other God but me' / I'll say I'll destroy the Temple and build it up again in three days / I'll plan all this for a Thursday arrest / If I'm not then betray me / Friday has to be the day of the hanging or it's not on / Friday eve being Sabbath they'll have to cut me down not to offend our laws / They can't have me hanging around on the Sabbath.

Disciples Right!

Jesus So on a Friday I could be hanging around for five maybe six hours and taken down presumed dead just before Sabbath comes in / On any other day I could be up there the whole fucking week / Then I'll really be pooped / Friday or it's not on / right.

Disciples Right!

Jesus So whatever you do, if Pilate comes out and says, 'Shall I spare him?' you must shout, 'No, crucify him!' You've got to / He's got to want to do it, now.

Disciples No.

Jesus He must feel there's a danger every minute that I'm alive / threatening the state / which he will / Mediocre people feel threatened by men with ideas / He'll want to do away with me that day / He'll need support / I have to be done away with that day / Others may shout to save me / your voices must be strong / Turn up early / boom in his ear / I've got to go on the eve of Sabbath or I'm a dead man.

Disciples Right!

Jesus You'll kill me unless you make him do it then. And that's on the same day / Now whatever happens don't let them break my legs / or I'm really fucked!

Disciples Right!

Jesus Don't let them break my legs to hasten my death / I'll look dead enough / believe me / If they ask / refuse / If my people think I'm not dying quick enough for the Sabbath and ask Pilate for permission for a leg break / refuse / Say 'Let him suffer / let his death be long' / No fucking leg breaking.

Disciples Let him suffer / let his death be long / No fucking leg breaking!

Jesus Or I'm in shit street, apart from the prophecy 'That not a bone of his shall be broken' / I'll never walk in three days and the plan is that in three days I must be seen walking / I must be seen to be believed / and I ain't gonna hobble along on sticks.

Disciples react with laughter.

Jesus I've gotta look new, risen from the dead / It's gonna be a bastard on the Big X / and it's gonna take me all of those three days to recover / I'd like a week / but Isaiah in the prophecies says three days, so three days it will have to be / I must fulfil scripture all the way / to the letter / plan it carefully / rehearse it / All right, what do you do with my clothes?

Disciple 3 'They shared my garments and cast lots for my clothing.'

Judas Psalm 22.

Jesus Then make sure they do / All right so they're bloodstained rags / but they'll be valuable in years to come to gory souvenir hunters / If they don't, offer to buy them yourselves as mementoes of your master / Then they will clamour for them / ask them to draw lots fairly and you pay the winner / Now one hour before Sabbath comes in I will say, 'I thirst,' thus fulfilling scripture Psalm 69.

Disciple 2 'And they gave me vinegar to drink.'

Jesus And you hand up the sponge / at the end of the stick / Put it against my lips / I will take but a little / the drug is strong, that is all I will need / Now this vinegar sponge is always there to relieve the poor friends on the cross / so no one will object if you pass me some.

Disciples Right!

Jesus The drug will effect a deathlike torpor / the cue for this will be sunset / one hour before the Sabbath comes in, I will cry / 'Eli Eli Lamma Sabacthani' (*My God, my God, why hast Thou forsaken me?*) / Then fetch Joseph of Arimathea / He will ask for my body / He will go to Pilate and explain that a Jew cannot still be hanging on the Sabbath.

Disciple 6 ~~Right we will do that.~~

Jesus Take my body down / and be never so careful when you take out the nails.

Disciple 5 ~~Right.~~

Jesus Wrap me in the white cloth with herbs / I shall be put into Joseph's tomb.

Judas Got you.

Jesus To make it look better roll a great stone in front of the tomb / The Pharisees fear the rising and will suspect / they will place a guard in front / Everyone knows by now my claim that I will rise in three days / They will wait / I will escape out the back through a secret passage /

Disciples (*laughter*)

Jesus While they guard the empty tomb for three days, I will be healing myself / I have only three days to recover / three / Everything depends on the rising / After three days they will open the tomb / empty /

Disciples (*laughter*)

Jesus They will scream / they will say that you stole the body while they slept / Now, if I can rise from the dead / why will my hands still have the nail wounds / still have holes in my feet / If I could rise from the dead why not renew myself?

Disciple 5 You needed the holes.

Disciple 4 You needed to show us that it was you.

Disciple 3 We didn't recognise you.

Jesus What, after three days!!

Disciple 4 You changed, how could you not, what with the hanging, the scourging, hours in the heat . . .

Disciple 5 Loss of blood and everything . . .

Disciple 2 And we couldn't recognise you.

Jesus Good, very good, so when I come out / refuse to recognise me / although I have told you umpteen times I will rise, you suddenly lose faith and don't know me / You Thomas will ask to see the wounds from the nails and to feel the hole in my side / Call witnesses as you do / make sure everyone sees / Afterwards pass the word / Go to Galilee / Go forth therefore and tell the world / I have fulfilled scripture / and be assured I am with you always / always and till the end of time / I just hope I do not bleed to death / That's the risk you have to take / I gotta hold on / If I can hold out we're away with royal flush / We've scored the coup and no one, but no one can deny his eyes / With that we splatter through the western world / With that we'll move our mountains / To come back from death is worth a million souls who'll follow once the word is out / Get witnesses and scatter ye throughout the land, they'll follow you like sheep / and those who don't – condemn them / Condemn them for ever / they'll change their tune once word gets out I've risen from the dead / You'll see my faithful men / You'll have an avalanche no sweat / You'll have them eating from your palm / You'll have them stomping in the aisles / They'll flock to you like shoals of fish / and hold them in your grip / I can't go through all this again / so blow it not / You know that what I'm doing is for good / not bad / Proclaim the news / tell those who believe – salvation awaits / unbelievers – threaten / Tell believers that if they drink deadly poison they will come to no harm / Tell them that / you know that what I am doing is for good / The Messiah will never come / so we have to create one / Gods are created by men / and men alone / the ingredients are there / It's all in the big book / Isaiah showed us how / Read the prophets / and bung a psalm or two in / Stretch a point to make it fit and voilà! you've got the Messiah kit! For those who want to try / this is the drill / It's not for the weak / the course is most severe / and many fall at the first hurdle / great planning and great strategy is needed / apart from staying power / You come through that, pal, and we'll listen to ya! / That's what I'm saying / Go through that and you'll get the mob / I'm going to Jerusalem tomorrow / let us hope we make the grade / Get those flowers and branches out / the rest / is . . . FAITH!

SCENE FOUR

Disciple 2 Spread the word. We know what we must do / I don't for sure / but think somehow / we have to change things – Yes, that's one way to look at it / so we walk and walk all day / a village / people working / The day grows cooler / returning from the demanding earth a farmer wants / to be with wife and child / What do I do? / Inflame him with new thought / a hand on his shoulder / *Yes?* / Spare me a moment, friend / *He thinks let me alone / but nods politely* / *What do you want from me?* / Tired / says his eyes / food cooking / smell of fat and herbs / His eyes wander / we talk of some man / he nods and smiles politely / smelling his food / mouth watering / baby crying / His wife / folded arms leaning against the wall behind / 'Don't be long, Aharon / your dinner's nearly ready' / He shrugs / *You understand he* *seems to say / wife works hard / eat while it's hot /* He looks at us now / our dusty dirty feet / dishevelled hair from walking, walking, walking / You know how it is / the warmth of family and hearth await his work-aching bones.

Disciple 5 In the darkening evening we stand outside, always outside / opening our mouths / open and close / He doesn't hear us any more / his mind is on the weight of crops gathered that day / on the price of aubergine / He sees our mouths moving, telling him prophecies and world events / *He listens for his baby's cry /* of blood and stones / of murders, trials / and parables / *he thinks will it be fine tomorrow / shall I thresh and winnow the wheat /* Arose three days later / *the baby's stopped crying /* Right hand of God / *God, I'm hungry, when will these bastards go /* Salvation in death / *My food is getting cold /* Your sins . . . / *Old fools! /* Cured the lame / Oh yes / made the blind see / *Coming Devorah /* The dead arose / *You must excuse me /* Angels . . . / *Stupid bastards / why don't they do an honest day's work /* Died for you / *Thank you I must /* Faith . . . / *must fix the baby's cot /* Can move mountains / *Must pick the olives /* The kingdom of heaven / *Coming, Devorah /* Is yours . . . / *Gentlemen . . . /* He died for you / *My wife is growing angry /* Son of God! / *My food is getting cold /* Listen to me! / *Goodnight.*

Disciple 1 It's dark / small fires are sputtering out / Inside it's sweet / with smoke of meat fresh killed and herbs / Soft woman's comfort in the night / and animals that nuzzle masters / growl at us / the village growing still / except a lizard twitching / a bat flicking past / and us walking / walking / always walking / sleeping in a barn sometimes / Not more / A child's voice crying in the night / or being newly baked in soft warm bellies / The glittering eyes of women / they stare hard at us / We offer less to them than they think / For women religion is a curse / that rules the lives of men / and not a blessing / How wrong they are to think we snare the souls of men for Christ / to build his army / God's army / Women view us balefully and never have us in the house to talk / but always by the door / or on the porch / outside always.

Disciple 4 The women make us feel unsure / for reasons we don't know why / Because they / each of them perhaps / are / in a way gods themselves / inside their bodies / they create / Yes / Don't like God's interference if you like / that bit does not go down so well / Virgin / They don't like that at all / Those that know the ebb and thrust of life / the seasons of the body / blood / birth / suckling / the heaving sex of their mates creating the magic paste that binds the future bone and flesh / It rankles in their instincts / closer to the instincts of animals / Virgin / That bit does not go down so well / They prefer to mate with husbands / not with God / Not have a child that's prophesied to endure nails that split and tear the tissue so carefully spun within their wombs / Not see the issue of their loins spread-eagled soaked in blood / The women do not like that bit at all.

Disciple 7 Can't see how it could be necessary that he should die for them / to cleanse the sins of them / of all mankind / A babe sleeps in her arms / one in a cot / a third pulls at her ragged dress / The bread is baking / her face shows daily toil / her hands red raw / her eyes search for what sins she needs forgiving / What sins / she says, what sins? / What sins! / Her eyes they look contempt and turn to ice / the door closes / we walk and walk / to tell the truth, I'm getting tired / To tell the truth I am / really tired.

Jesus Keep on, Faith, you gotta have faith, look what

MESSIAH

I'm doing for you / I'm dying for you / I know it's hard for you / It is for me / We must spread the word / the time is running out / the final test is still to come / What is a nail like through the hand / a soft hand / a hand that heals / that likes to touch soft things / that likes to hold / that likes to spread its fingers / Be gentle / hard pointed nail / through the skin / veins and bone / splinter / through my hand / How long, nailed like a butterfly to a stick / how much blood can I lose / nailed through the feet / That bone is thick / my bones are large / Will I walk in three days? / after a nail has rammed and cracked through these feet / found its home in the wood / thud! / How long does it take to smash a nail into a living bone / solid bone / through both feet / and I must walk on these bloody raw feet / in three days I must / swollen broken / cracked / How long can I endure it? / How long can I? / How long must I . . .

Chorus You'll find out pal / It's coming to ya!

Disciples It's Passover / let's eat / It's Passover / let's eat / somewhere good / but where / a decent nosh / no rubbish / It's the last one / He'll know a place / Trust him to know a place / He can pick and choose / course / he can pick and choose / course.

SCENE FIVE

Flesh and Blood. Last Supper.

Jesus Eat my flesh / drink me / I am the bread of life / My spirit / the spirit alone gives life / therefore my bread is my spirit / My flesh is of no avail / it is the words which are both spirit and life / Eat my words and you drink in my spirit / I'll make you eat my words and you shall live forever / Don't act like the dried-up hypocrite priests in their cold, dank temples who pretend it is my body / and my blood / you are not barbarians and cannibals / understand a parable when it's thrown at you / don't be shmucks all your life / Bread is of no avail since it perishes / I am real food / the food that keeps you alive forever / the food that helps you sustain your soul and spirit / Hence I am flesh and blood to you / in my deeds, in my words / drink them in / take me in you / The priests will try to take you away from me / They will say don't do this / don't do that / while claiming authority from me / They will use my name like counterfeit money / They will make you bend your head to them in huge palaces / when you should bend your head to no one but your true God / You will kiss their hands / admire idolatry / they will wear costumes that bloat their importance / They will appear like gods in their jewelled vestments with dirty undergarments / They will glitter with their precious gems while thousands starve / Hypocrites and vipers they are / They will make small gestures as if all powerful / while their bodies are trussed up and diseased / They will enjoy vile habits and preach to you self restraint / They will have power to remove you from the church forever / which only your God can do / If I came back they would throw me out / but from my heart they will never remove you / In this temple you will always be safe / there will always be a space there as long as your thoughts travel direct to me unweighed down by earthly things / Pray to me even in your rooms and I will come to you / I will not show myself in palaces for they are built for man not God and are abhorrent to me / I will not show myself to the rich / they revolt me / I will not glance at those who sit on thrones and make the poor suffer / they shall perish and wither / I will not show myself to the arrogant for they think themselves as gods / I will not show myself to the envious / these appal me / I will not show myself to the greedy for they steal from others / I will show myself to none but those whose thoughts are clear / I am the bread of life / my spirit gives life / Eat me!

Disciples Nice one, Jesus!

SCENE SIX

Judas Money / I keep the money / I'm the cashier / that's me / the pilferer, keep accounts / cream a bit from off the top / that's what they say / dabble in the dirt / That's too holy for his holiness to touch / raise funds / drop a shekel here and there and grease the greasy shabbes goy / be the fall guy / thirty pieces! / Don't make me laugh / He gave me the bread / a bit like a pitta / crossed with a matzo / arm outstretched / a bit of hummus dripping off the end / his eyes fastened to mine / like he would draw mine out of my skull / a crooked little smile on his face / Like, it has to be someone / so why me I thought / Everyone's staring now / the hummus is dripping on the table / I take it from him / they all watch / can I swallow the thing / Damn if I can / it sticks in my mouth like a cyst / like a growth / I get up / Oh well let's get it over with / I've swallowed it / I'm outside / in the air / It's good to be outside / the atmosphere was getting oppressive in there to say the least / Imagine / all twelve of them talking about death / I've had it up to here these last weeks I can tell you / Maybe he knew that / that's why he picked me / There's so much you can take and no more / It smells good out here / even more so in relief after that / Who needs it / all this talk about betrayal, burial, death, sorrow, more death. You'll do this / You'll do that / You'll disown me / You'll betray me / You'll kill me / This one will do that to me / I wanted to say / 'Give over / you're getting on my tits / If you want a prophecy off the top of my head' / I was dying to give him a bit of slagging to tell the truth because much as I admired him / all this me, me, me, me was hurting him / It got so he couldn't think of anything else / A mouthful of aggro might have straightened him out a bit / got him off the self-pitying number and back to work / But I didn't / I was scared of the others / their gooey eyes hanging on the ends of stalks / their long tongues lapping up and writing down every word he said / so I kept shtumm / It smells good out here / everything smells of pine / It wasn't a bad dinner up till then / I like the Passover / I like the matzo and the ceremony / the bitter herbs and the lamb / Very suitable time to be topped, eh, the sacrificial lamb of Passover / He's no mug / I start to run / it's getting quiet / everybody safe behind their doors playing nicely with the family . . .

Disciple 4 Drinking the Passover wine / saying the prescribed prayers / the fathers wrapped in white prayer shawls white as snow / playing with the children . . .

Disciple 1 The children hearing the story of the passing over of the plague which left the Jews untouched and the firstborn of the Egyptians slain . . .

Disciple 3 Until Pharaoh had to release them / just had to / No Jew was touched that besmirched his doorpost with the blood of a lamb.

Disciple 7 The angel of death said / 'No, not that one / they're one of us.'

Disciple 2 The eyes of the children glisten in wonder as the father tells the story the way his father told him / and they in turn will tell their children as the mother serves the meal.

Disciple 6 The beaming Passover scrubbed faces of the children / the soft murmur of prayer / like a velvet drone over the city /

Judas Only me outside running like a lunatic / sweating like a pig / plotting like a snake / cunning as a rat / Inside the houses I pass / peace and warmth of the family / oil lamps throwing the shadows celebrating on the walls / The exodus /

Disciple 3 And now they tell the story unaware of another story being formed / being acted out this very moment.

Disciple 1 The city's at peace / the Romans relax / no Jews to give them hassle tonight / no riots to put down.

Disciple 2 All quiet, not knowing that outside is the beginning of their end / The mad shadow running is another angel of death . . .

Disciple 6 Only this time there is no blood on the doorposts / Little does he know what he has set in motion . . .

Disciple 4 The wheels are turning / soon to be the rack.

Disciple 3 What has he set in motion? / Had he known / he had rather not began . . .

Disciple 7 Had rather never opened his mouth . . .

Disciple 2 Had rather been struck dumb . . .

Disciple 1 Had rather never been born . . .

Disciple 5 Had he known what he had set in motion . . .

Disciple 4 If he could see the rivers of blood pouring away in his name . . .

Disciple 3 If he could hear the wailing of the children that he loved . . .

Disciple 1 If he could hear the crying of the mothers . . .

Disciple 6 The screaming of the daughters . . .

Disciple 7 Could smell that sickly burning of the flesh in his name.

Disciples How could he not know that!

Judas Prophet where are your prophecies now / you who see the future and read the past / *Give me my money!*

End of run.

Priests (*chorus*) You'll wait, you'll get it brother. You'll get what's coming to you!

Judas He's in the garden of Gethsemane! (*To Caiphas, then exits.*)

SCENE SEVEN

Caiphas. A Priest. The church loves ceremony.

Caiphas Who is he that speaks thus? / He must be killed / Shut the mouth that pours out truth / or we will drown in it / Our power is protected by a solid wall of ignorance, thick with prejudice, lies and stupidity / Truth is a flood that gathers and builds and breaks down the wall so he must be stopped / that's the way of things / Our laws are precious / without laws we cannot impose our power and our punishments / People come to us with wide eyes / He claims to be the son of God / they squeal / yet he wears rags / Blasphemer / kill him / People like uniforms and dressing up / In fact the less internal authority you have, the more you need outward show / We are the servants of forces higher than he / we must be recognised / we have our duties / our laws / we must always support the state / they support the army / without them how can we hope to convert the ignorant races to the blessed words of God / This way the people are enslaved to the kings and queens / and religion binds the state together / To create anarchy stop religion / stop believing in your state god and the next thing you know you'll stop believing in your king or leader / So religion binds the state the way no party can / It stays, it lasts and people die for it / without it they have only the soulless state, with it they have love and a promise of life everlasting / if they are good, that is / (*Removes outer garments to reveal modern priestly garb.*) Besides I love the ceremony, the mumbo-jumbo, the pomp / dressing up / ivory and myrrh / I like gold crucifixes stabbed with rubies as if dripping with clots of blood / pearls and sardonyx / I like incense and damp / I like the sweet flesh of marble saints / and ivory tears forever cascading down alabaster cheeks / The swooning songs of choirboys and their piercing untesticled sweetness – the shrieks of angels are not sweeter / I love the chants in the echoing vaults of great cathedrals / singeing the buttresses with their virginal laments / I love the children who sing of him in their white seraphic sweetness and to caress their delicate bodies / behind the altar / I adore the drone of the mass / the sunlight splintering through the stained glass where he forever lies oozing his blood in the frozen crystal / I love the portraits of the saints with tilted heads / their beautiful slim bodies caught into an expression of pain as arrows nuzzle their way into their intestines / I love the children / I love their sweet dangle of flesh before it is corrupted / I love the widows scraping their knees onto the dust begging for redemption / eyes turned up in hope / moist large innocent / My hem being kissed / my ring being kissed / and I kissing the rings of pink cherubs / I adore the angels / I adore the voices of the people / the poor and the ignorant begging me to forgive them / confessing their filth to me / I love my people / even their filth / and if it's good, especially their filth / I can hear the hearts of women pounding in the confession box / pounding I hear them through the thin walls as each struggles to tell me all / I drink it in / I eat the words / they fill me up in joy / I empty myself and anoint the earth / my cup runneth over / I wait for more and the choir swells in hallelujah / as she sings the praises of her sins / and I eat it up / every drop / and I forgive her / and the statues even blush to hear / they squirm in the renewed agony / The paintings seem to renew their clots of blood / the wafer becomes flesh in my mouth / Oh holy sweet flesh / his body I can taste in my mouth / and can I not taste his hot salty sweet blood wafting down his flesh / Oh, Oh, Oh, my God! I do love you / Oh, I love thy body and blood in me.

SCENE EIGHT

Before the Court.

Priest 5 He's here.

Priests That's good.

Priest 6 Will the charge stick?

Priests Like shit to a blanket!

Priest 3 Enough for the sentence of death.

Priests Not many!

Priest 2 What's he say?

Priests That he's the Son of God.

Priest 7 Tell me another . . .

Priest 1 And that he'll be sitting on the right hand of God.

Priests That's blasphemy!

Priest 6 Are you the Son of God? Eh! Big mouth.

Priest 2 If you're so flabby with your gob, play the prophet now, Jew boy.

Jesus Look, these are the passages that refer to me. See here, this and this . . . That's me, this bit here and here and this one. Yes, that's me too . . . You see, all right and this / Now are you convinced? / You fools, faith is what you need / You gotta have faith / but you have faith in nothing but your doubts / Don't question so much / Don't be dumb / What do you want, facts? / Here they are / here and here . . . Look, look at this bit here / see . . . That passage . . . Never mind the buts, it's close enough / Don't question what you see staring you in the face / The prophets showed you, / said I'm on the way / what more do you want? A letter of recommendation? / If I tell you, you'd better believe it / If you don't beware / you'll die in your own sins / Believe me I am the light of the world / I am God's son / I will lay down my life for my father and receive it back again / I am the shepherd who lays down his life for his sheep / No one has robbed me of it / I lay it down of my own free will / I have the right to lay it down and receive it back again / Whoever comes to me will never be hungry / Whoever believes in me will never thirst / I am the living bread which has come down to you from heaven / If anyone eats this bread he shall live for ever.

Priests Kill him.

SCENE NINE

Questioning in the House of Caiphas.

Priest 3 He says . . .

Jesus I'll destroy the temple / in three days / rebuild it.

Priest 2 Fuck you pal / we like the old one.

Priest 7 You wannim?

Priest 1 Nah! You can have him.

Priest 6 Crucify him / according to plan.

Priests Good.

Priest 5 Too many following him / danger to the Roman state.

Priest 4 Faith makes martyrs.

Priest 8 He's a good guy / too bad . . .

SCENE TEN

The Last Journey.

Disciple 4 He's on the way / the cross is heavy.

Disciple 5 Wait / he stumbles.

Disciple 1 There's a volunteer / Thanks pal, you'll get a credit.

Disciple 7 It's hot.

Disciple 2 It's Friday.

Disciple 3 The houses are being cleaned for Sabbath.

Disciple 3 He's lain on the cross.

Disciple 2 The first nail selected.

Disciple 5 In the left hand / of the man who must punch it home.

Disciple 7 He pauses.

Disciple 4 Holds the nail's point carefully.

Disciple 6 On the palm.

Disciple 3 Is this centre?

Disciple 1 Yes . . . / Right hand lifts the hammer.

Disciple 5 It's / gone very quiet / fuunnyy . . .

Disciple 7 The birds stopped / not / a murmur.

Disciple 2 Not / a breath.

Disciple 4 Even the clouds / hanging still.

Disciples Ouch!!!

Disciple 1 He doesn't flinch.

Disciple 6 The second nail.

Disciples Ooooohh!!!

Disciple 3 A small gasp.

Disciple 7 Sound of splitting wood.

Disciple 4 His eyes turn up.

Disciple 5 Like he heard something / like you do / when a friend / calls from a window.

Disciples Oh no!

Disciple 1 A huge jet / nail hit the main line.

Disciple 6 It's pouring out.

Disciples Ah shit / shit.

Disciple 3 It's spouting like a fountain.

Disciple 7 He looks down.

Disciple 2 Now he looks worried.

Disciple 4 Looks sick.

Disciple 1 The faces around look sick.

Disciple 5 A lot of blood.

Disciples Oh shit.

Disciple 2 The nailer shakes his head.

Disciple 6 He's not pleased.

Disciple 3 He finishes the feet.

Judas Under the red rainfall.

SCENE ELEVEN

This is the Last Thing.

Jesus You know what I'm doing is for good / so tell it anyway / just like the plan / So what if it didn't work / the intention is the thing / You know what you must do / spread the word / My time is running out / You know that what I do I do for love of you / Love makes the world revolve / so tell it like we said / leave a space of time before you set all down / say that I rose again, just like the good book says I would / and if I don't survive, let time dissolve that little fact / witnesses will die / but legends last forever / My spirit will live on / and that you know / What use is flesh and blood / it's to no avail / my spirit is the fire / so fan it well / keep it alight / and spread the flame in every heart / Do it with love / with gentleness / Don't be cruel / be kind / I love you / I'm afraid / Where's my mother? / I thirst / Oh God / Why hast thou forsaken me? / It's over.

Soldier 2 Is he dead?

Soldier 6 I think so . . . He was the top honcho, right?

Soldier 3 Yeah, so?

Soldier 6 Well, they'll pay a few bob won't they . . . I mean for his clobber . . .

Soldier 3 Course! Like they're mementoes yeah, I mean they're fucking like holy relics, yeah. I mean we could get a few bob for them, especially in Rome.

Soldier 6 You could be right, now you're using your nut.

Soldier 2 I'll play you for them.

Soldier 1 Bollocks! Do it a bit at a time . . . OK, throw for his sandals . . . (*Throws.*)

Soldier 6 You're jammy you are, bastard! OK, for his tunic.

They throw.

Soldier 5 Not your day old son, ha ha ha . . .

Soldier 6 Sod ya, ya bastard . . . OK, his fuckin' crown? . . .

Soldier 2 What! That bloody bunch of twigs on his nut . . .

Soldier 6 You never know . . . it might be worth a few bob one day . . .

Soldier 2 Nah, you can have that . . .

Soldier 6 Oh ta.

The End.

OEDIPUS

Introduction

My version of *Oedipus* seeks to examine the play and occasionally peer beneath the tendency to strut and pose, to high-blown rhetoric and an air of self-importance somehow unavoidable in versions of Greek tragedy. I also sought to relate some events to images of today since the greatness of Greek tragedy is that its themes deal with the power of natural forces and the cycle of life and death. So its shadow lies across the years and its arguments are mankind's into perpetuity.

I see Oedipus as a modern man, self-made, tough and bold, who uses language as a weapon to cut through verbal adiposity and obliqueness. He is more of a strutter whose stance relates to him having always to battle against some force determined to defeat him. Whether at the crossroads where he destroyed his father and the officious guards, or the Sphinx, he seeks to combat fate and leaves his adopted home so as not to fall into its predicted trap. So when yet another problem in Thebes raises its many heads Oedipus is already fight-trained to deal with it. He is seldom destined to have peace, to win a battle and rest on his laurels, and it would seem that fate has dealt rather cruelly with him.

What is incredible to contemplate is a crowd of seventeen thousand spectators in an open air theatre coming to see and hear a cycle of dramatic performances and the only thing one can compare this with today is a rock concert where an equal number would gather for an event which, although utterly divorced from the complexity and dynamics of the Greek ritual, nevertheless, at its best, has its own ritual. Its songs celebrating universal passions and dealing with love, life and death. The crowd today are as involved and the proceedings have also a ritualistic air. The performances are larger than life and amplified no less than the Athenian theatre performances that were amplified through the masks of the actors.

The Oedipus story is the star turn in all the Greek tragedies and was probably Sophocles' best and most popular – certainly one of the most performed. This is apparently also the judgement of Aristotle who had the play constantly by his side, according to the splendid introduction by E. F. Watling to his very serviceable translation.

I have chosen to attempt my version in iambic pentameter for the main characters since I feel they must have the sweep, the flow of verse. Also the meter contains and strengthens their position. What the spectator wanted in the fourth and fifth centuries BC was epic drama whereby mankind's own fate can be held up for examination. For dissection. A kind of operating table revealing the innermost parts of the human soul. Mankind in all his elemental nature pushed to his limits as if the drama was some kind of severe testing of the product called a human being. However, the ultimate test is whether mankind can bear the rigorous testing of moral law. Here we see Oedipus tested to the utmost and eventually made to pay the terrible price. It is a harsh price since he really is absolutely innocent of any premeditation of wrongdoing. A good lawyer today would plead mitigation to all charges and even put it to the defence that he was 'set up' which in a sense he was. It was a 'fates' set up.

It is his supreme arrogance, his refusal to even contemplate anyone else's point of view or their 'truth', which eventually condemns him.

Characters

Oedipus
Priest
Priest 2
Creon
Tiresias
Jocasta
Messenger
Shepherd
Second Messenger
Chorus

Oedipus has not yet been performed.

Oedipus

Children, children, flesh of my flesh, blood of my blood,
Speak your hearts to me that overflow.
You cling around my feet like creeping vines,
As if I could protect you from your woes.
The city groans like some poor wounded beast
That I'd pick up and stroke and heal its wounds,
And could I *not* do so much more for you.
With mine own eyes I came to get the facts,
No messengers to tell me second hand,
While I sit back behind my desk and nod,
And scratch my head and pass a few more laws.
I'm out here on the streets and face to face,
So speak old greyhair, you are the wise man here,
And fill my ears with your dread tales of grief.
Your eyes have shrunk to sunken holes, poor man.
So let me, King, chief and head of state,
Blow away those ragged clouds of fear
With one great puff of regal power, so
Tell me man, let's hear the rattle of your throat!

Priest

King Oedipus, great sovereign and lord,
You witness young and old and those between.
Mums suckling new-born brats who pray
Their sprats will grow to full-grown men
And in the market-place are offerings burnt
To gods of fire, earth, and air since they
Have broke their bonds to keep the world in harmony.
Now look upon our city, see the storm

That batters down the streets in rains of blood.
The fruit is twisted and rotten on the tree
As well as blasted in our daughters' wombs.
A plague rot fever stalks the town
Pouring its filthy breath into our lungs
Until black bile spurts from our very mouths
Where once we bewitched our wives with songs.

Priest 2

That is why we bend and chafe our knees
Before you, master of the universe,
Commander of men and a bridge to those
Who live above our human misery
Who ride upon Apollo's mighty steeds.
You have their ears, remember it was you
Who freed the city once before, great king,
You pried the talons of the filthy Sphinx
From round our throats, silenced her riddling tongue.
So Oedipus, our most venerable chief,
We cry, we beg, we all kneel down.
Oh rescue our good city once again.
A word from you just whispered to the gods
Will carry far more weight than all our prayers.
Or else, your own high-flown intelligence
That soars upon vibrations in the air
May catch a clue, the way you snatch a gnat
That's buzzing in your ear.
So be a king of men and not of ghosts.

Oedipus

Grim news, my children . . . yet not new to me.
From my own bed I heard your nightly cries,
I could not pull the sweet blanket of sleep
Over my head, nor sink into oblivion
Since each new cry would pierce my heart.
You did not wake a dozing man, my friends!
Our city's cursed with some noxious malaise

Yet none so cursed and sick as I, who bleed
For you, the city, and myself.
So tortured in mind and soul, my wife Jocasta,
My great Queen and I did clutch at straws,
Anything to find some answers here,
Come on! Let's put some strong wind in our sail.
We'll navigate these troubled seas my friend
And find safe harbour soon, I promise you . . .
Yes, easy to mouth metaphors I know,
They're only words to put some stiffness in our spine,
Some oars to row us when we are becalmed.
So now I've sent for Creon, my Queen's own brother
To sniff the ground where great Apollo roams.
At Delphi, home of oracles, he'll find some clues,
Who knows, some angry god's bearing a grudge,
Or someone here forgot to pay his dues.
No matter what the cost we'll make it up,
OK? Appease the gods, wipe clean the slate.
When Creon comes, the instant he arrives,
Whatever the demands are from the boss
I'll to it straight, no fear, no compromise,
Or 'Can we please negotiate the deal,'
Renege on words that have been stamped and sealed.
It's peace we want, security for our state!

Priest
Now these are the words we love to hear.
And bang on time, for look, your brother Creon appears.

Oedipus
His eyes glow brightly, see his heaving chest,
He has that special sweet smell of success.

Priest
He looks a winner who flicked the dice
And it's come up nicely, double six!

Oedipus

Just hold your horses, hang onto the reins,
We're at the starting gate, not won the race.
Hey brother, what's the news? We burst to know.
Just spit it out, we're ready for the worst.

Creon

Favourable, our wounds will surely heal.
And one day when they're fading scars,
We'll point at them and have a rare old laugh . . .

Oedipus

But how and when and why and what to do?
You torment us with mystery, we want hard news!

Creon

Do you want the world to hear, so every mouth
Will tell the story according to their fears?

Oedipus

Speak out to all, the collective ear,
It's just as much for them as you and me.

Creon

OK – no sweat – I'll give it to you straight . . .
He says, cut out the monstrous growth within
That feeds and fattens itself on the body politic,
Like some vile cancer feasting on your limbs.

Oedipus

Ha! But how, what medicine should we apply?
What treatment will cure this dread disease
That spreads its pox upon the public face
Like shiny pearls waiting to suppurate!

Creon

Banishment, or else a death for a death.
The city frets, a splinter in its flesh
Festering a septic poison, pull it out . . .

The criminal who shed the precious blood
Of great King Laius, slaughtered like a dog.

Oedipus

The murder of King Laius is the cause?

Creon

It is a crime unsolved and must be purged,
Its sin stinks up the land just like a corpse
Left rotting and unburied in the sun.

Oedipus

I know he was a much respected king,
My ears are never empty of his deeds.

Creon

He was a goodly king and just to all
Headstrong and bold and not unlike yourself.

Oedipus

Sometimes my wife doth make comparison.
I shrink beneath the legend of the man!
But sadly never had the chance to meet.

Creon

The killers live and breathe and must be found,
We must catch the assassins, blood for blood,
By drawing theirs, *our* blood will then be pure.

Oedipus

But where, they could be any place on earth,
The crime's turned cold, why didn't you sniff it out,
When his gore was hot upon the stones?

Creon

The city was in chaos and the Sphinx
Distracted our attention with her crimes.
Besides, some factions live for anarchy,
Festering like rats beneath the streets,
But when the dread assassination comes
Watch how they crawl out of their cracks and squeak!

Oedipus

So find a needle in a stack of hay.

Creon

The god said here! . . . It's here! Seek and ye shall find.

Oedipus

What *here*!? The killer boldly struts and gloats!
Were there no witnesses to the event?

Creon

All done to death except just one who fled
From highwaymen, at least that's what he said.

Oedipus

What else did he describe, give me some clues?

Creon

'Daylight, cut down, a robber's pounding clubs,
It's hot, sun's blinding my eyes, the dust is rising,
The horses shriek to a halt, rear, we jolt forward,
Horses paw the ground, sneering at the bit.
Through the haze, a man or men standing
Grinning, outlined shadows, the light smacks your
    eyes.
Breathing horses, otherwise deadly quiet.
A shout, the echo bounces off the hills
Returns mocking the King, its owner's ear:
"Get back, get back or else you'll feel my wrath!"
A naked blade is drawn, bright dazzling, the King's.
The robbers, bandits grin, spittle shines their lips.
A crow wheels in the sky, the sun's behind them,
Outnumbered, their clubs rise and fall, rise and fall
Just like they were cracking walnuts.
I turned and fled and didn't turn back to look.'
That's what he said, those were his very words.

Oedipus
Anarchists hungry for power paid a bribe
To carry out this crime of regicide?

Creon
But then why vanish into thin air and hide,
Not take advantage of the headless throne?

Oedipus
Perhaps they plan to catch me off my guard
While journeying on behalf of the affairs of state.
The rats that crawl out of the drains at night
Will always seek an opportunity
To bite us harder when we are asleep.
Therefore the cause of Laius is also mine.
So let us once again pursue the scent,
We must not rest nor tire till we have found
The snake and pulled it from its musty lair.

Priest
Children rise, the King has raised our hopes,
And we have heard Apollo's mighty words
That ring inside my head like thunderclaps,
Now we must act to end this foul and cruel curse.

Strophe One
Apollo spake, the golden voice
From Delphi's shrine
We celebrate.
Oh give us hope
But what's our fate
We faint with fear
By what we'll find.
A thousand sorrows
None can decipher.

We're given the answer
The evil is here

But how will we find it
And where will we look?
We can search for ever
But people are dying
Our faces are riddled
Our soft skin is rotted
Afraid to touch lovers
Dead babies delivered
The graves overflowing
The pus ever flowing
The tears always flowing
We melt in our acids
Our tongues turned to bile
Our boils big as hives
Our blood thick as glue
Our seed turned to dust
Worm-eaten we rust
Eyes covered in crust
We awake every morning
Eyes open in fear
What will we find?
Examine our loved ones
Is that a *new* swelling
Was that *mark* always there?
Or is it the light,
A shadow that's crawled
Over your face?
I close my eyes
But then I hear
Your breathing is quicker
The rasping of air
As life struggles through
The waterlogged lungs
I cover my ears
To shut out the sound
The sound that you make,

That you make as you drown
I close my eyes
I shut off my ears
But then I feel

Your chest against mine
Your heart beating loudly
Pounding and pounding
Telling me something
Escape from this place
This place of evil
The heart pounds against
The walls of its cage
Wishing, oh wishing
It too could escape . . .

I close my eyes tightly,
I block off my ears,
I move from your body
But then I smell,
I smell the dead bodies
Outside in the carts
I smell the dying
I smell your own death
I close my eyes tightly
I block off my ears
My hands are clasped hard

Hard tight to my ears
I block up my nose
I sleep all alone
Away from your dying
Flesh and your bones.
Away from the pounding
Fist of your heart
Beating faster and faster
Until it must burst.

Now all is silent
I fall into sleep

I dream of your dying
I see your face swelling
I feel your heart pounding
I hear your lungs drowning
I cannot escape

I leave my lone bed
I unblock my nose
I unclasp my ears
I turn to my loved one
I sponge off your sores
I hold you so close
I share your pain
I feel your heart fading
But you die in my arms
Not lonely in sorrow
Not empty and cold
You die in my arms
A smile on your lips
And I will soon follow

I awoke the next morning
And I spied a swelling.
Was that always there,
Or is it a shadow
Formed by my hair?

Priest

Oh champion Apollo, help us,
Send us fiery shafts of hope
Shot out from the great sun's bow,
Oh Bacchus, god of bursting life,
Let us drink the wholesome vine.

Oedipus
That's it! Pray your guts out till you gasp!
Then listen . . . absolute mercy is at hand.
Now hear my master plan to halt the plague,
My knowledge of the crime, of course, is slight.

Chorus
Oh yes, that we know!

Oedipus
I need some clues to track the killers down,
So I address you all as man to man,
No beating about the bush, so hear me straight . . .

Chorus
Oh, we're listening . . .

Oedipus
One of you, just one soul knows the truth.
So ventilate your secret, heave it out!

Crowd
Oh . . .

Silence then murmuring.

Oedipus
Don't fear for your skin, my friends, you'll be OK.
There's gold for you, don't try to think,
Don't use words like 'informer' and 'betray'.
Don't hide some filthy scum who shares your blood,
Brother or sister, cousin or in-law.
Or, 'I'm not a dirty spy, I'm not a sneak.'
Now that's a misconception of the truth!
If anyone gives roof to the assassin
Or nourishes the beast within our midst,
Just hear this, pay attention and take heed
'Twere better that he never had been born,
I'll cut him off from all human embrace,

No ritual, speech, sacrifice or even mate
Shall warm his heart or sweeten his sour bed.
Thrust out from our embrace this man will be
A symbol of the pestilence . . .
A brand I'll stamp upon his loathsome head
So folks will point at the foul fiend and say,
Get out! You hideous lump of wretchedness,
And whip him from their hearth with thongs of steel
And children will throw stones and spit
At this disgusting traitor's wickedness.

Chorus

Yes, yes, yes, that's just the way,
You said it, sir, that's fair enough, I'd say.

Oedipus

And *I* will take the medicine I prescribe
Since if by some wild chance the villain hides
Within the royal palace, close to me,
Then on myself I'll invoke every curse
I just proclaimed . . . This I do swear,
And no man was or could be more sincere.

Chorus

We hear you King and so believe in you!

Oedipus

I'll do my best to pay for your neglect.

Chorus

Neglect?

Oedipus

Yes, neglect to solve a monarch's death,
I hold his precious sceptre in my hand,
I sleep the good night in his bed,
My bed of seed, and am good children blessed,
They could have been his rightful progeny,

I share his wife with him, untimely dead.
Such ties in blood oblige me to revenge,
Just like a father would be by his son!
I shall not rest until I purge his death
And find the tyrants that dared slay a king,
The son of Labdacus
The son of Polydorus
Heir to Cadmus
And those that choose to disobey this edict
I'll beg the gods to curse their fields
That nothing there will ever grow but weeds
And wombs condemned to fructify with freaks!

Chorus
Sir, we will not perjure our good selves
By filling the air with evil lies
But do exonerate ourselves from sin,
We know not who the killer is,
Apollo hinted he is here within
So let him point the culprit out.

Oedipus
We cannot order gods about
To do our dirty work
'Point the villain out,
We'll sit back and watch,
Oh thank you god . . .
We'll be in touch
Next time there's trouble,
Please send the bill.'
He shows the way
Like when you're lost
You ask a stranger
Where is the place
He points the way
You don't expect him
To hold your hand

And walk with you! . . .
Be brave and put
One foot in front
The other will follow.
We'll find the place,
The journey's good
To teach us something
So they say.

Chorus

Send for Tiresias, though born blind,
He sees the secrets within men's minds.
The man sees all, his tuning fork
Will pry the bad vibrations out.

Oedipus

Twice have I tried to reach Tiresias
But oracles march to a different tune.
Let's hope his tuning fork will vibrate soon
While there's some alive who give a damn!

Chorus

Oh don't speak like that,
You gave us hope,
Investigate
Each clue, each tale.

Oedipus

You are the smart one here, so you begin.

Chorus

To start, the old tale
Some say it smells,
Some, a cover-up,
That he met his death
By travelling vagabonds.
Well, villains always make
Ideal fall guys

When there's more at stake.
But it's a start
And there's a witness too.

Oedipus

I want that witness re-examined now
Squeeze him a little just in case
There's some flavour left for us to taste.

Chorus

He'd be a bold one sure to sleep at night
With your curses eating inside his brain.

Oedipus

Words will not halt the beast that kills,
Evil cannot hear the sounds of pain.

Chorus

Here's one who hears the sound of human woe,
The holy prophet comes, a living fount of truth.

The old and blind Tiresias is led in.

Oedipus

Welcome great mystic, visionary, scribe,
Though darkness hides your eyes, you see
Far more of what men try to keep inside.
You feel, I'm sure, the city's agony.
You, wise old man, are our last refuge now.
Our dearest wish, hope and prayer too
Is that you'll shed some light in these dark times,
Apollo, bless the god, showed us the route.
'You want deliverance from the plague,' he says,
Then extirpate the very cause of it,
The king killers who live within our midst.
The earth is cursed while they do live on it,
You, who can hear the grass grow, have the skill.
On you, the visionary, turns the world,
You are the eyes and ears and senses of the time,

Save us from this dread affliction, please
Save yourself, the city and save me.

Tiresias

What suffering might I bring to end the pain,
The surgeon's scalpel hurts to make a gain
I'm not sure I'm the one to wield the knife.

Oedipus

What makes you now so full of doubt?

Tiresias

The blade, once in, might bring more things to light,
So let me go, believe me it is better so.

Oedipus

Call that an answer, to refuse to speak?
The city hangs upon your every word . . .
You leave the people more confused and bleak.

Tiresias

You want fair words, then try to frame your own
To be persuasive, King, and much less terse!

Oedipus

By all the gods, do not deny us now,
We bend our knees, please tell us what you know
I'm ready, I can take it, spit it out!

Tiresias

Vain King, the hard foundation of your house would
   shake.

Oedipus

You mean you know the cause and will not speak?
You'd let the city die in pain and ignorance?

Tiresias

The pain would overwhelm us both my King,
Don't let the monster out of his cage, I plead.

Oedipus

> What monster, do we have another Sphinx!
> Don't yak in riddles, prophet, speak clearly now.
> Or maybe it's just possible that our wise old seer
> Doesn't possess an iota of an idea!

Tiresias

> I look inside your heart and see what's there!

Oedipus

> Hear that! I mean that's gall, insult your King
> Because it's plain to see he doesn't know a bloody thing!

Tiresias

> It will out in time . . . I need not say it now!
> I've had my say so spit and rage away.

Oedipus

> Don't worry, mister, I don't intend to waste
> My energy on fakes and charlatans.
> You've conned your way too many years, old pal.
> A bullshit artist! Go on, take a hike!
> Before my anger tempts me to be rash.

Tiresias

> Oh, is that your well-considered plea?
> Then you shall know . . . you spit against the wind.
> The very curse you trumpeted to all
> Is sliding down your own imposter's face!
> From this day, pack your bags and leave this state.
> The rotten canker that you seek to cut
> From out the city's guts is inside you!

Oedipus

> Say that again! I can't believe, I can't believe your hate.

Tiresias

> No hate moves me to speak, from truth we grow.

Oedipus

It staggers my imagination so . . .
Speak it again . . . just keep the message slow.

Tiresias

I tell you, you're the murderer that you seek!

Oedipus

The man's insane, I'll have you bound in chains!

Tiresias

The knife's in now too deep to pull it out.
Shall I reveal the other loathsome growth?

Oedipus

I'm fascinated, mouth away your fantasies . . .

Tiresias

I say that you and your beloved wife
Are wrapped in sheets of a most hideous sin.

Oedipus

Just like the venomous snake it needs to bite!

Tiresias

The truth will only hurt the ones who hide.

Oedipus

'Truth!' is a filthy word your mouth secretes,
Blind man no less in mind than in your vision.

Tiresias

Remember those last words, they'll be *your* epitaph.

Oedipus

You foul degenerate thing that lives in night,
You can't soil me, I'm clean, live in God's light!

Tiresias

Don't rail against the wind, it's to no avail,
Remember Apollo's words: 'Search your own house!'

Oedipus (*to Chorus*)
    Oh how I've reaped rewards I never asked
    You put a royal kinship in my fist . . .
    What loathsome envy has my fame inspired?
    Ah Creon, was it you my 'loyal' friend?
    Did you go creeping behind my back
    Slavering to stick your ugly arse
    Into my throne by witchcraft, grab and snatch?
    Conspiring with fairground fakes who read your palm
    And probably feeding him the lines . . .
    You fooled the people all this time, my friend,
    But when it came to pass the acid test,
    The Sphinx exposed your sad magician's tricks.
    Where was your vision *then* on which you're famed?
    Asleep of course, since you're the village fake.
    Yet I, a simple man called Oedipus,
    Had something that we sometimes call 'street wise'
    But now the snake desires to crawl inside
    The palace with King Creon by his side,
    Ah you will see how your own villainy turns on thee.

Chorus
    Oedipus, you speak in wrath
    It muddles up your wits
    Your mind is sharp
    It's been the cutting edge
    Upon which many foes
    To their deep cost
    Have deeply bled.
    Don't blunt it now,
    Acid rusts the blade.
    Just let him speak,
    Since what he says
    Is based on signs from birds.
    An old technique
    But if not

He'll hang himself
With his own words.

Tiresias

To clench your fists does not become a king
Nor to raise your voice, love only knees that bend.
Forbid the truth to scour out your house,
Afraid in case a little light discovers
A rattling skeleton in your cupboard.
I am a king, I reign over my tongue . . .
That is my subject who demands an equal say.
The weakness of your wit stoops to the ground
And, childlike, mocks the fact that I am blind.
But I say *you* are blind outside and in,
Blind to your birth, blind to your origin,
Blind to the hate that's sleeping in your bed,
Blind to the curse a dying father left,
Blind to his widow's prayer to avenge his death.
One day their words will be like pointed thongs
And lash you all the way to your exile
And you will spend your days in endless night
Tormented by ugly dreams that will not fade,
The horrors stored away inside your brain.
So I can hurl abuse as well as you
Except my words sting with the ring of truth,
Don't they, Mr King?

Oedipus

Gods, must I listen to this loathsome thing?
Slide back, you slug, beneath your darkened rock.

Tiresias

You called for me, I never would have come.

Oedipus

That is a stone that I should have left unturned!

Tiresias

You grew to be a fool and yet born wise . . .

Oedipus
    What know you of my parents since you know all!

Tiresias
    This day will be the answer to all your quests,
    I'll take my leave, your hand, boy, let us go.

    Takes hands of helper.

Oedipus
    Your riddance is a blessing in my eyes!

Tiresias (*turning back to him*)
    Then let your blessing be delayed a while.
    This man you hope to smoke out with your threats
    The thug who shed the blood of good King Laius
    This killer you will recognise at once.
    Be patient, King, and you will shortly see
    The unravelling of the murder mystery.
    You want some clues? He's Theban born and bred,
    Fathered two children and became their brother . . .
    A son became a husband to his mother . . .
    The same son slaughtered his own father . . .
    So chew on these words for a little time,
    You're very good at riddles, so you boast,
    But if I'm going at too fast a pace,
    Next time you primp before your looking glass
    You'll find the answer staring you in the face!

    He exits.

Chorus
    In Delphi there is a stone that speaks
    Will it track down a man
    His crime not purged
    Quivering in his secret den
    Knowing the fates are closing in
    His hours marked in grief,
    The criminal mind

Is never free
Guilt chews through
His broken sleep
His acid sweat
Eats up his floor
Digging a hole
For his grave.
The seer's words
Cast a cloud
On Oedipus.
He cannot confirm
He cannot deny
It's insane, a great big why.
There was no quarrel
Between the men
This is not a killer king
Made mad by greed?
Or a sneaking dirty thief?
Or a man who lusts for power?
He defeated the Sphinx
He risked his life.

Who is the witness?
Apollo knows.
Is the prophet infallible?
No man is.

I'll not judge
Before the proof.
Find the evidence
Not hot words.
Anyone can shout and spew
But I'm uneasy
I'll not convict
Oedipus! Guilty?
It doesn't fit!

Creon

Good citizens, in haste I fly to acquit
Myself of this monstrous charge, this lie
Thrown at my feet by Oedipus the King!
It stinks like some foul piece of rancid meat.
It will distract a starving dog or two
But you know me, could you believe
Not in your wildest dreams I would deceive
The King, commit one act that has a taint
Of something dirty, underhand, unclean?
I'd rather die than have my life stained by
This most unjustifiable and filthy crime.

Chorus

The charges were made when tempers were affrayed.

Creon

It's said that I colluded with a seer
And paid him to poison the city's ear?

Chorus

We cannot comprehend why it was said
But here the master comes . . . let *him* confess.

Oedipus

Oh, bold-faced wretch, how dare you step
Inside my door, murderer, king killer!
Were you slobbering to take my place?
Audacious, why you've got some bloody neck,
Some guts, to think that you could take me on,
Or is the drug of power just too strong?
Some people are so hungry for the royal cloak
They'd stop at nothing, choke their own grandmother,
Sell their children into slavery or worse.
There is no deed too foul they would not do
To woo the smiling waving universe.

Creon

So tell me just what is this crime of mine?
Tell me some facts, don't just rant and whine.

Oedipus

You urged me to send for that insane seer,
But tell me, how many years since Laius died?

Creon

Some fifteen years, or just a little less.

Oedipus

And was this prophet spouting his lava then?

Creon

He was, and honoured far and wide.

Oedipus

But at that time he failed to speak of me?

Creon

That's right, your name never did pass his lips.

Oedipus

And yet you did investigate the good King's death?

Chorus

We did sir, low and high
And high and low.
The killer seemed to disappear
Into the sky.

Oedipus

Then why, oh please reflect, did not your wise man
Then stride out and scream it to the world
And point his scabby finger in my face!
Ha! Silent? Sure!

Creon

That I can't begin to answer for.

Oedipus

Now fifteen years too late a little bird
Sits on your shoulder, whispers in your ear . . .
Or is the bird my tweeting brother-in-law?

Creon

Why? Why should I want the aggravation,
My status is assured behind the scene,
I am rewarded, rich, and want for naught,
A tranquil mind, respected by my peers,
A lovely wife who graces all my days
With children perfect stamped with her own seal,
Why should I jeopardise my treasured realm
To grasp the nettle of the kingly woe?
No, and once again it's No! No! No!
A tranquil mind does not desire strife
And treason is a strange commodity.
Go on man, and put me to the test
Visit Delphi, beg Apollo's voice
'Are Creon's words a lie from the traitor's mouth?'
And should the impossible be true, that you,
Should find a confirmation from above
That I did plot your fall with fortune tellers
Then snuff both our lives out in a flash.
You're killing even now the sweetest friendship . . .
And what is life without friends, cold and bare?
Cool down the brain, you must take time to think,
Don't saw the branch beneath your very feet!

Chorus

He makes some worthy points, I would beware
Of jumping to swift conclusions, sir.

Oedipus

Swiftness prevents the rot from settling in,
Deliberate too long you give the enemy time
To plan and execute his plots!

Creon

Like a rabid dog you bark and fret.

Oedipus

A dog that will not hesitate to bite.

Creon

So self-certain, so cocksure you're in the right.

Oedipus

What's right!! My life stands evidence for me.
For fifteen wholesome, happy, peaceful years
I lived a life in blameless sweet content.
And now you hurl these deprecations on my head!
Fifteen long years later you decide
Now the state is sick, unsure and weak,
That I am guilty of the crime of regicide!

Jocasta (*has entered*)

You wretched fools, how absurd men behave
Who have been gifted with full-witted brains
What shame to argue like embittered foes
When all around the land is dying, slowly
Gasping, begging, howling for the truth
While you two spit like raging alley cats.

Creon

Spit you say, his venom's from a snake!
Your husband wishes now to extirpate
My face from this entire land and ban
Me from my rights, my life or instant death.

Oedipus

For plotting 'gainst my person, 'gainst a king
My wife, you know the penalty for treason.

Creon

God strike me dead if I'm a guilty man.
Poor creature, the plague has made you lose your reason.

184

Jocasta

    Oedipus, my brother treads the narrow path
    You hear, he's made an oath to God
    To strike him dead if he's not pure at heart.
    When has he lied before, deceived, betrayed?
    When? How? Give an example, search your mind!

Oedipus

    Hate gives birth to monsters when it's time,
    And not before, but now the country's chaos
    Tempts the rats to invade the city's gates.

Chorus

    Never a friend betray, or else disgrace
    Since friendship is your love for man and faith.
    Accuse a friend, you then accuse yourself.

Oedipus

    So, let's put down our cards upon the table.
    Would you prefer *my* banishment or death
    To cure the plague, perhaps a change of face?

Chorus

    Now God forbid such thoughts
    Let Helios burn
    Set me on fire
    Extinguish me to dust
    Till I'm a mote
    A speck that floats
    In our country's sour air
    If such craven thoughts
    Sit in my head.

Oedipus

    So I should let him go, that's what you want?
    Perhaps you think, that would appease the fates?
    I therefore abrogate my harsh demand and spare
      his life

So he may spread his filthy lies like fleas
Upon the city's pale and rotting flesh.

Chorus
Choose to forgive and then you cannot hate,
Your anger's like a storm that has to rage,
Now let us see the clouds pass from your face.

Oedipus
Out of my sight, your cringing begging tongues
Are like a constant beating drum inside my head!

Jocasta
Oh Oedipus, my darling husband, King,
Tell me what has thus provoked you so?

Oedipus
Willingly, but sadly too, my wife,
Your brother Creon seeks to destroy our lives.

Jocasta
But why, tell me clearly, what's the cause?

Oedipus
It's insane, unbelievable, you'll gasp,
I can barely shape the maniac's words
Between my lips.

Jocasta
Just calmly, tell me now.

Oedipus
He makes me . . .

Jocasta
Yes? . . .

Oedipus
Me, your loving and devoted husband . . .

Jocasta
Yes, yes?

Oedipus
Me, who risked his life to kill the Sphinx . . .

Jocasta
Yes?

Oedipus
Me, who served my country these long years . . .

Jocasta
Yes, yes?

Oedipus
He makes me . . . the killer of King Laius!

Jocasta
Oh my God! What evidence has he got
To make this charge?

Oedipus
None but a foul-mouthed seer
Who vents the thoughts that Creon planted there.

Jocasta
Then let me, darling, heal your bloody wounds
Since legends, lies and malice, like keen whips
Have bit into my darling husband's flesh.
There is no art of prophecy, I have facts!
Facts are hard and fast and certain proof . . .
Once long ago, there came to Laius an oracle
A man all kings by habit desired to meet,
Naively believing in strange signs,
In how the birds do shape their morning flight,
The shrill they make returning to their nest,
Or even read their crap upon the roof.
As I would guess, since kingship needs some help,
To ease the weight from the incumbent's neck.
The madmen claimed that Laius would meet his fate
At the hands of our own precious child, no less!

And, King Laius, suspending kingly judgement,
Leaves our son, just born, a babe three days!
To perish, ankles tied, just like a peasant's unwanted
    sin!
And yes there was a murder, Laius was killed
But by some unknown bandits, some murdering scum
That scour the highway where three roads meet . . .
There you see, the oracle cannot make
You do the things that they prognosticate.
King Laius' son never did kill his father,
What will be is made by your own acts.
The stars are guiding lights for God's great journeys,
Not dice with which he gambles with your life!

Oedipus

My own dear wife, each word has struck a chord,
A memory buried deep within my mind.

Jocasta

What memory have I disturbed?

Oedipus

Laius met his fate you say, where three highways
    merge?

Jocasta

That's how the tale is told.

Oedipus

Three highways where? Where did the act occur?

Jocasta

Where the road from Delphi . . .

Oedipus

Meets the road from Foccis?

Jocasta

But that you knew, you asked me once before . . .

Oedipus
How many years ago?

Jocasta
Just some short time . . .

Oedipus
. . . Before I came to power?

Jocasta
Yes, the news was scattered everywhere.

Oedipus
How we are the playthings of the gods!

Jocasta
What is it, husband, what dreams are now awakened?

Oedipus
I can't reveal the pictures in my brain.

Jocasta
Your wife will take the pain, extract it like a thorn . . .

Oedipus
If only you could; King Laius, tell me his age,
What shape, what look?

Jocasta
Tall, his sable hair was streaked with silver.
In looks, gaunt, strong, an eagle's piercing eye,
In form, not far removed from you.

Oedipus
Oh my God, I sink into a pit
So deep I cannot even see its depths.

Jocasta
Where are you now, my love, what pit?
Hold on to me, I will not let you fall!

Oedipus

A pit so dark and inescapable,
I am afraid now of the eyeless one,
What has he seen in that infernal gloom?

Jocasta

Nothing! Only the fear he planted in your mind.
Tell me, Oedipus, and I will pluck it out.

Oedipus

I'll try to paint the picture once again,
Help me fill in the details, my dear love.
Did Laius set out on that fateful day
With his usual bodyguard of men?

Jocasta

It frightens me to tell you anything!

Oedipus

Just tell me that . . .

Jocasta

Five men there were in all, and one the herald.
Just a single chariot for the King.

Oedipus

I sink again into a pit of snakes!
My wife, who told you of that horrid hour?

Jocasta

The one man who escaped the bandits.

Oedipus

Yes, 'the bandits'! Where is this witness now?
Is he alive, still in this house perchance?

Jocasta

No, the man was much distraught with grief
For failing to defend his honoured lord,
And when he saw you reigning in his place,

He begged, on bended knees to leave the state,
And live a shepherd's life far from the sight
And memory of Thebes.

Oedipus
To see this man is now my greatest need!

Jocasta
How will he help to fill the details that you ask?

Oedipus
Certain things are best left in the head,
Bad seeds will always find a fertile earth.
Words once out, spread like the canker,
They need no compost, just foul men's breath.

Jocasta
But me! Cannot you trust your words to me?

Oedipus
Oh yes, my darling, for I will need your strength
To help me climb from out this hellish pit.
So share with me the story I shall tell.
My father Polybus and my mother Merope
Were the foundation of my youthful life.
They showered me with love unquenchable,
Through them I grew into the city's foremost man.
One day a loudmouthed drunk was overheard
To say that I was not King Polybus' son!
His royal blood did *not* course through my veins.
I fretted all that day but dared to ask . . .
'Tell me, tell me the truth of who I am,
Am I the true and only issue of your love?'
Yes! Yes! and Yes! again they said,
Each yes a hammer blow upon my doubts.
But still a tiny worm of doubt remained
For me to kill, to stamp on for all days.
I fled to Delphi, to the Oracle.

'Tell me what I need to know,' I cried,
'I beg you lay the truth down at my feet.'

Chorus

'Poor man accursed
Kills his father
His creator,
Returns to the womb,
The womb of his maker
Where he exits
He enters
His progeny accursed.'

Oedipus

'Why, why must this be, why choose me!'

Chorus

You were not chosen,
It is luck,
A game of dice.
Some are accursed,
Some born to suffer,
Some live long lives,
Some children die,
Some are afflicted,
Some, perfect blooms,
Some are born rich,
Some born to be poor,
Who is to say?

Oedipus

Why, why must this be, what have I done?
Determined to avoid this destiny I fled,
A year did pass before I stopped my feet,
Before I dared to shake the dust from off my feet.
I stood, the very spot where three roads meet,
And as I stopped and wondered which to take,
I heard a shout . . . 'Out of my way!'

Imperious, like a blow it stung my ears.
I turned to face the owner of that sound,
A man like you described, tall, silver-haired,
A horse-drawn chariot, stomped and reared.
The groom, he tried to run me off the road.
I threw him to the ground with his own whip
With which he tried to inflict on me his master's wrath.
Silence – only the panting horses and this man
With silver hair who stares, and even now
Recall the way he fixed me with his eye,
As if to fit a piece of jigsaw into place.
'No, don't, old man, I do not wish to hurt,'
But he, rising, raises a double-pointed club
And brings it crashing down upon my head.
A glancing blow but then I felt a flow
Of blood, a trickle curling down my cheeks.
Silence – he smiles, his guards, now they smile too.
Why, why don't you go, we've traded one for one,
But no, a second time, he lifts his arm!
Oh no! Not twice, old man . . . I broke his skull
With one swing of my stick he fell,
And where he fell . . . there . . . he . . . lay . . . down . . .
   dead!

The others, rushing in to embrace his fate,
Joined him at once, I killed them all,
Except the groom, who still lay panting on the ground.
There, the picture is nearly complete . . .
Is Laius the unknown nobleman I slew?
And like a dirty thief, I grabbed his wife,
Her husband's blood still on my hands . . .
The pit yawns open wide again for me
In which to hurl myself and dive down deep,
Accursed by God and man and banned forever
From human contact, friendship, and your love,
And that could be the cruellest blow of all.

Banished, like a filthy leprous thing,
Hell-born wretch and murderer of a king!

I want to fly but where, there is no place . . .
The dreaded curse still hangs over my head,
To cause my father's death and wed my mother,
My father Polybus, where not an hour
Passes in which I do not see his face,
I'd rather become a hermit in some cave.

Chorus

By what you say, my King, you were a pawn,
A victim fate embroiled into its net.
You did not set out to kill the King,
Your hand was guided by some other force
And acted by the rules of self-defence.
But wait until you've heard the witness speak.

Oedipus

Now my life hangs upon a herdsman's words
And I must sweat it out until he comes.

Jocasta

What can the herdsman say to ease your fears?

Oedipus

His words could be a knife to cut the noose
That's slowly tightening around my throat.
His words, please God, will free me, if they match
    yours!

Jocasta

What words, my love, what did I say?

Oedipus

You said that *several* bandits struck him down!
That's what you said, those words proclaim me
    innocent,
If he confirms those words, those precious words,

194

Then I, alone, did not commit the crime,
But if, oh horrid word, if he describes
A solitary man where three roads meet
Then the chasm opens wide its jaws again!

Jocasta

Never can that herdsman undo those words
He wove into our ears so many years ago.
The whole town gathered in the square to hear
His story and men wept and bowed their heads.
The day a great king dies no one forgets
But even, let us say, catastrophe . . .
And lightning strikes the herdsman on the way,
Did not your insane oracle predict
King Laius' death would be by a son of mine?
And he, poor darling, long ago did die.
After this I'd laugh at prophet's visions
Reading sheep's entrails or twinkling stars.

Oedipus

I'd love to share your optimism, wife,
Your female wisdom blows away the clouds
And superstition crawls into a hole.
But let me hear the herdsman nevertheless.

Jocasta

He's on his way, but let us rest
From all this grief and old wives' tales,
Let me look after my troubled boy a while . . .

Chorus

The law is
A radiant light
It shines on all our flaws.
The law is
The sun that warms
And heals.
The man who thinks

He's above the law
Stuffed with pride
Power drunk
Stumbles in darkness, blind
Disobeys his own eyes.
The law is
Like a river, flowing
Feeds the parched
And hungry earth.
Sins dam up
The precious flow
Then famine, sickness
And death follow.
I bathe myself
In God's laws
I cleanse my sins
Purge my mind
Wash the greed
From my hands
Scour my heart
From petty needs
I could not pray
Could not fast
Unless I believed
In Apollo's words
If the Oracles
Are turned to lies
What can we believe?

Jocasta (*re-enters*)
No, no, I have not lost belief
But must beware too many messengers.
Each one anoints himself the mouth of God
And now I fear there are too many mouths
And in the babble cannot hear his sound
That will unlock the mystery for Oedipus.

He only hears the high-pitched shrieks of fear
My words are drowned out by their cries!
Why are men so eager to accept
Bad things that only fill them with distress
As if sweet joys, like happiness and love
Are merely toys, that soon are torn away.

Messenger (*arrives*)
Good sirs, where is the great King Oedipus?
Please guide me to the palace where he reigns.

Chorus
You're there, good messenger, and here's the Queen!

Messenger
Heaven shine down on you great blessings, Queen,
The perfect wife for perfect Oedipus!

Jocasta
And blest be you sir, for your kindly words.
Let's hope the news you bring is no less sweet.

Messenger
Oh I bring news, Madam, to make you sing . . .

Jocasta
Thank God! I'll sing all night if it be fair!

Messenger
Well, it be bittersweet as well.

Jocasta
Suddenly my throat is tightened up.
Just let it out and swiftly now.

Messenger
King Polybus, the sire of Oedipus,
Did die a peaceful old age death.
And now they wish King Oedipus to reign.

Jocasta

I knew it! Yes I did, was I not right?
Too many mouths were jangling in his ear,
The forecasts of the gods I spit upon! . . .

Oedipus

Jocasta, my own love. There is some news!?
My heart beats like a drum pounds in my chest.

Jocasta

Listen to this man . . . just speak again.

Messenger

Your father is no more . . . King Polybus is dead.

Oedipus

By murder or by some disease?

Messenger

A gentle puff of wind . . . down falls the leaf.

Oedipus

Aaah! Poor man, my dearest, loving father,
And yet such sweet relief for all my fears!
Away with delving into Pythian oracles . . .
No fortune-tellers reading birds on high
What will be will be, don't wish to know
What footsteps I will take in ten years' time
In case, in trepidation waiting, I trip
Headlong and break my neck. My father's dead!
And sleeping soundly in the earth, unharmed,
While I stand here, my sword still sheathed,
Or did I kill him so with grief?
Perhaps he pined away to see his son!
But grief and murder are not stablemates!
Tiresias! Where are your accusations now?
Sell them in the market-place for dates!

Jocasta

I told you darling . . . Did I not tell you so?

198

Oedipus
> Jocasta, I was sick with fear and dread
> That fate should prearrange my life
> To make me kill the man that *gave* me life?
> But then the prophesies have still another half,
> The filth about my mother's bed!

Jocasta
> As false as is the other half, which said,
> You'd kill a king to get into your mother's bed.
> How many men have dreams of mother marrying,
> And dismiss them in the morning's cleansing light.

Oedipus
> All good sense, all perfect, Polybus dead,
> And yet my mother Merope is still alive.

Messenger
> How can this old and gentle lady frighten you?

Oedipus
> There was an insane prophecy that I . . .

Messenger
> Don't tell me if it cannot be divulged . . .

Oedipus
> It's over now and fate has lost the race!
> Apollo prophesied that I, a son,
> Would couple with my mother, kill the man
> The gods ordained should be my father.
> This put me far from my dear parents' eyes
> A cruel blow, never again to see your mother
> Nor glow under your father's swelling pride.

Messenger
> This is the fear that made you flee?

Oedipus
> Yes, this most wretched prophecy.

Messenger
Why wait, I'm bottled up just like a cork
About to pop and scatter sweetest wine.
And just one sip will cure your worries, King.

Oedipus
Ah, that would be a wine I'd like to drink.
No price could ever be too high!

Messenger
You fled because of this strange prophecy?

Oedipus
Yes again! Now spit out what you know.

Messenger
But wait, you were afraid, did you not say,
In case you did besmirch your parents' nest?

Oedipus
Yes, yes, I'm always haunted by that dream.

Messenger
Then let me put your mind and soul at ease.
Polybus was not in fact your father, King.

Oedipus
How could you utter such an insane thing!

Messenger
Because it's true, he gave you love, not life!

Oedipus
My father called me son, he worshipped me!

Messenger
You were a gift from God, not your father's loins.
Polybus took you happily from my arms.
You see, he had not children of his own.

Oedipus
So who am I, from whence did I arrive?

Messenger
You were discovered in a wood in Cithaeron.

Jocasta pales and moves away.

Oedipus
Good God, man! On Theban hills, you found me
there?

Messenger
That's where I used to tend my flocks.

Oedipus
Ha! A shepherd finds me in the woods!

Messenger
And luckily, I was your saviour, son.

Oedipus
You were, God bless you, and I am so grateful.

Messenger
Your little feet were tightly bound like a chicken
Trussed up to face the slaughterer.

Oedipus
Yes, that ancient pain I sometimes feel.

Messenger
I loosed your feet and massaged your small limbs.

Oedipus
I have the mark still on my foot.

Messenger
Poor swollen foot! Your new father said,
Holding you up with such joy in his eyes,
You were a prize from heaven, he said, and wept!

Oedipus

Swollen foot, the name did seem to stick.
Who left me there to die as food for wolves?

Messenger

This I do not know, the man who found you,
He could tell, most like, your origins.

Oedipus

Ah! Not found by you but given second-hand?

Messenger

You were discovered by another shepherd,
He begged me to find you a loving home.

Oedipus

Where is the shepherd now, please tell me who?

Messenger

He was a herdsman for the late King Laius.

Oedipus

Another link, we'll soon find the entire chain!
This herdsman, is he still around you think?

Messenger

Your own good people best could answer that.

Oedipus

Speak out if any of you know that man,
Or seen him in the hills or in the town.
Gold I'll throw to him who gives a name.

Messenger

But sir, it was the selfsame herdsman,
The very man you asked to see before.
Jocasta here can be the judge of that.

Oedipus

Come my wife, is this herdsman our missing link,
The survivor of that murderous attack?

Jocasta
> Why dig into the ashes of the past
> Like some street cat that seeks for mouldy scraps?
> Forget it, darling, it's not worth it now.

Oedipus
> Forget it! When it's the evidence we need,
> One link to complete the entire chain?
> And then I'll wrap it round the oracle's neck!

Jocasta
> For God's sake it's enough, I can't hear more!

Oedipus
> I need to know from whom and whence I came.
> Who cares if I'm the love child of a slave!
> Every being needs to know their roots.

Jocasta
> I'm warning you, it's folly to proceed.

Oedipus
> Can I believe that you're afraid of truth?

Jocasta
> If truth will cause you more distress.

Oedipus
> So you like wandering in the dark?

Jocasta
> Yes, I'm begging only for our happiness!

Oedipus
> If truth were perched on top of Mount Olympus,
> I'd crawl on hands and knees through broken glass.

Jocasta
> Then crawl back to the man that you once were,
> But when you find him, God help you my friend!

Oedipus

Where is that wretched herdsman, bring him here!

Jocasta

Farewell my love and poor deluded man . . .
I have lost you twice and you are damned!

Oedipus

What does that mean, 'you've lost me twice'?
Because it may be proved that I'm a peasant,
Left to die by some poor frightened slave.
As many do like babes were surplus fruit
That's thrown out for the birds to feast upon.
And now the Queen is mightily ashamed
To think her bed was by a slave's son stained.
I do not blush to own my motherhood
I will embrace and love her, her who gave me life.

Chorus

Who's your mother?
Where is she?
A simple woman
Lost in love
The father gone
Alone she wept
As she set
Her bundle down
On the mountainside
As do the poor
When they are
Big with child
No maids and slaves
To celebrate
The warm new life
No, she must go,
Snuff out with tears
Her own light

That pours from out
Her bleeding heart.
Oedipus, we celebrate
The precious light
That was not
Blown
Out!

A figure, old and rough, enters.

Oedipus

Look, my senses tell me, that's the man,
The herdsman we've been seeking, the final link!
He's old enough and matches this old man.

Chorus

We know him from afar, King Laius' servant.

The shepherd is ill at ease. Oedipus scrutinises him.

Oedipus

I ask you carefully, Corinthian,
Is this without doubt the man you mean?

Messenger

The very same, there is no doubt.

Oedipus

Good sir, I thank you first of all your pain,
Now tell me straight, were you in King Laius' pay?

Shepherd

Yes sir, born and bred to serve the King.

Oedipus

How, in what way did you serve your lord?

Shepherd

Chiefly as a shepherd, sir, tending his flocks.

Oedipus

Good, then you came across this other shepherd here?

Shepherd
What mean you, sir?

Oedipus
Come, the man who stands before your eyes,
Did you not meet him once before?

Shepherd
Ah . . . that I couldn't say, not now, for sure.

Messenger
Then let me jog the old boy's memory,
You can't forget those wooded slopes of Cithaeron,
The smell of pine upon a summer breeze,
Where we did crouch sharing some wine,
Good neighbours for three long sweetened years,
Now tell me fellow, am I right or wrong?

Shepherd
Ah, yes, you're right, but it was long ago.

Messenger
Now you must remember this, old friend,
Don't you recall a tiny baby boy,
You thrust into my arms, 'Please keep him safe . . .
I can't just leave him here to die, I can't!
Each precious life is like a miracle from God,'
And tears were streaming down your face.

Shepherd
What are you saying . . . what are these questions for?

Messenger
Then take a look, the child you nobly saved –
Is standing there, he was that precious babe.

Shepherd
You are, I think, a little more than crazed.

Oedipus
Be careful, shepherd, guard the words you say.

Shepherd
Great King, what have I done that's wrong?

Oedipus
Refused to confirm what this man has sworn.

Shepherd
The man's mistaken me for someone else.

Oedipus
I'll squeeze the truth from out your ancient throat!

Shepherd
God help me, sir, what is it you must know?

Oedipus
Did you give the man the babe, or no?

Shepherd
I did, I did, I should have let him die!

Oedipus
Let me die! How dare you, vile old man,
Regret now your single act of charity?

Shepherd
I was commanded to let you perish,
But as you see, you're breathing, live and strong.

Oedipus
Who gave you such a dread command
That you at least with honour did countermand?

Shepherd
Before one word more leaves this head, please
Pull my tongue from out my throat instead.

Oedipus
I'll tear you rather limb from bloody limb
And let you slowly bleed to death, now speak!

Shepherd
You came from the house of Laius, my Lord.

Oedipus
At last! A slave perhaps, a reckless interlude
The King might wish to hide?

Shepherd
Yes, something like that, my Lord.

Oedipus
Something's not quite the link that fits!

Shepherd
The Queen, perhaps, may have the piece you seek.

Oedipus
The Queen! *She* gave the child to you?

Shepherd
Just as you say.

Oedipus
With purpose to do what?

Shepherd
To kill it . . . get rid of the damned thing!

Oedipus
The child's own mother?

Shepherd
She said, 'Oh God, I cannot succour my own babe,
Why have you cursed this innocent thing . . .
I wish that I could die instead,' she cried . . .
'If that would take the curse from off its head.'

Oedipus (*slow, wretched realisation*)
What have you done?

Shepherd
I saved you out of pity, sir,
But now I see my pity was misplaced.

Messenger

    If you are the man he says you are,
    Then Oedipus, poor man, you are condemned!

Oedipus (*credo*)

    Why should a man be chosen to obey
    His fate stamped out and preordained.
    I struggle to escape, think I am king
    Of my own destiny, *I* shape the world!
    Or does the world shape me to fit a plan,
    Of which my struggles are like a fish that leaps
    Into the great bear's mouth or frying pan . . .
    I chose my wife or did the gods place her
    Upon the path where we would surely meet.
    Since they can read the seeds of time,
    Did they wish to play a cunning game,
    To put me just like Theseus in a maze,
    And watch from high me trying to escape,
    Laughing like children tormenting flies . . .
    And am I their amusement, a living toy?
    No more, no more, I will curtail your joy,
    Now *I* will be the master of my fate,
    I will no longer witness what you've done,
    I take your world away.

    He exits.

Chorus

    Vanity and nothingness
    Is man's destiny
    Swollen with fantasies
    He strives vainly
    Always to be
    The mirror's faithful effigy.
    He does not see
    The glass decay
    Before his eyes

He feeds the mirror
Silver baubles
Silken robes.
Where the glass
Has sucked his flesh
He paints the shadow
In rosy tints
And squints to see
If overnight a tributary
Has new emerged
Running from the river
Of his eye.
He cries to see
A silver thread appear.
He plucks it out
Only to find
The next day
Three new silver friends
Are ensconced there.
Now he is afraid
To stare harsh truth
Back in the face
He sits instead
Counts his wealth
Coins don't decay.
He counts until
His back is curved
His eyes barely see
The treasures piled so high
They shut out the light.
The blazing sunsets
Pass him by
Stars are useless
Flecks of dust
The purple dawn
A nagging light

The man decided to face
The unrelenting mirror
But there are two dark holes
Instead of eyes.
He is happy now
To see
The world outside
Is always night.

Chorus
Poor Oedipus who navigates
The selfsame stream from birth to man.
Who ploughed his own father's soil
And sowed the seeds from whence he came.

(*Alternative*)
A warning sign
Do not disturb
Nature's laws
Or chaos comes.
Plague, famine, war,
Hurt nature,
It bites you back
Hard
Where it hurts most.
Oedipus cannot be blamed
He's an example
That we should learn,
Respect God's laws
But God is nature
Not man
What you plant you reap
That's all.

New messenger arrives.

Messenger
Listen, my most honourable lords –

If you can stand the pain, if not,
Then stuff your ears and hide your eyes,
Disaster upon catastrophe, bad news
Chases its friend just like a lover pursued.

Chorus
There is no agony that hurts
A body already flayed and whipped
So let's have it, mister, and quick.

Messenger
I'll tell it quickly so quickly hear,
Jocasta, our dear Queen is . . . dead.

Chorus
Oh no . . . This grief we did not hope to hear
This news has found an unmarked place
To inflict new welts onto the city's face.

Messenger
By her own hands she wrenched her life,
Bursting through the bedroom doors she cried,
'I cannot hope to see my son again,
I cannot hope to touch my husband's face,
I cannot hold my children any more . . .
Oh, my darling ones, forgive, forgive!'
Then, she howled, she cried, oh she did rage,
Tearing at her precious silken skin,
She carved out vicious grooves that quickly filled,
Called out just once the late King Laius' name,
Then thrust that royal head into a noose
Using the selfsame silken sheets
On which they had so peaceful laid.
The final act I could not bear to see.

All eyes were on the raving Oedipus,
We hear him shouting down the halls,
'Where is that putrid breeding ground, my bed,
From whence I made my entrance on this earth,

And yet the beast returns to till the bloody plot
The criminal returns to the scene of the crime.
Jocasta, what do I call you, Mother, Wife?'
Then coming to the bridal suite
He shoves the double doors into a hundred bits
And then explodes a shriek that can be heard
Even by the gods who must have paused.

Oh then we saw the horror behind the door,
For then we saw the final scene unfold,
Her, hanging, dangling, twisted, dressed in gold.
He, mouth agape, sucks in the air like panting beast,
Eyes wide, unblinking, as if he wished to paint
The painful image in his tortured brain.
Unties the noose and lays her gently down,
Just like a lover with his virgin bride.
Then . . . his hands gripping her shoulders, lowers
    his lips,
And . . . gently imparts a lingering farewell kiss.
But . . . then, just then, just in that loving moment,
He . . . pulled from off her golden dress the brooch,
The pin he held 'tween finger and thumb
Then thrust it swift into his precious orbs
Again and yet again, and one more time –
A double fountain gushed with scarlet rain.
Yet . . . even then, yes, even then he speaks,
'At last, oh sweet darkness, at long last!
I sentence myself to perpetual exile,
I can no longer see my wretched shame,
Blind for so long with open eyes,
I tear them out, those wretched parasites!'

Great Apollo, are you satisfied now?
Open the palace gates that all may see
The wretched perpetrator of their misery.
The criminal found out, exposed and tried.

Poor man, the tower of strength is crumbled now,
The Colossus battered by unceasing waves,
Shakes, trembles, then in one long shudder, breaks.

Chorus
Man of woe
Blinds himself
Self-punishment
What for,
To gain a
Deeper sight?
Pain and misery
Is this the lot of man.
Is this the bitter fruit of guilt
What for?
Exile, banishment,
Wasn't it enough?

Oedipus (*enters, wounded and bloody*)
Friends, it was Apollo who made this be,
My sins spread like maggots in a garbage bin
And so I took away my sight, why not?
There is nothing left I do wish to see,
I do not want to see a fresh dawn rise
Without my soulmate breathing by my side,
Nor glimpse the stars' eternal nightly ride
Across the heavens without her sweet embrace,
Nor taste the morning fruit without her face
To face me each and every day . . .
And so my eyes are useless to me now
Since there is nothing left I can enjoy.
No friends, no welcome smiles into their hearth,
But eyes frozen in horror, loathing me,
The God-detested man.

Chorus
Endure your fate, bear it bravely now.

Oedipus

Cursed be the man who cut my bonds!
Curse him for untying my fettered feet!
Curse him for allowing me
To walk to my accursed destiny, curse him!

Chorus

Enough, enough, perhaps it would be better
To live no longer, than in darkness.

Oedipus

Enough? Enough of you and your advice,
My act was good, it cleansed the world for me,
I need no eyes to gaze upon my father's face
Or my unhappy mother's in Hades' halls,
Or eyes to see my sins engraved
Upon my poor children's innocent faces
Or eyes to see the city I cast away,
No, none, rather I should plug my ears as well
And dam the river of the world's great sound
Until I am a carcass, blind, deaf and dumb.

Chorus

Creon, thank God you came, to ease his woes.
Please take control as guardian of the state.

Creon enters.

Oedipus

I have no words, Creon, strong enough
To rebuild the citadel of love
I butted down with my thick skull
When I was blind with my own arrogance.

Creon

I am not here to feed upon your sorrow
Nor flay you with bad memories of the past
Nor shove the words back in your throat.
The gods have thrust your face in your own muck

Therefore escort him swiftly to his home
Where only a family's ear and eye should see
And hear a family's intimate tragedy.

Oedipus

No, no home, no warmth, no smell of past.
Dear Creon, bless you for your clemency
But you must throw me out and quickly too,
The way you kick a mad dog from your door,
Lest it infect you with its loathsome bite.
So kill me, go on, strike me dead,
Kill the arrogant beast, the parricide.

Creon

It is not for me to do this thing.

Oedipus

Then give leave to bury my dear wife
With everything we ever shared or loved,
Give her a tomb befitting of her state.
For me, this city Thebes must never see
My face again . . . thus will the curse be lifted.
The sores and blemishes will swiftly dry
Once the disease is plucked from out the city's eye.
For me, I'll go back to my childhood hills
And there I'll while away my allotted time,
Away from the sounds of human kind.

Creon

Poor man, is there not one thing in the world
To aid your solitary journey?

Oedipus

Yes, Creon, and bless you for asking me,
My children. Let them be cared for, never shunned
For what was never any fault of theirs,
My sons are strong, I know they will fend,
But please protect my little orphaned girls,

Sweet birds that sang to me at every meal,
Shared everything I ate with them,
Their joyous laughter was my daily feast,
Just once I want to touch them, one last time.

Creon goes off to fetch them.

Creon, you generous King, grant me this thing,
To hold my darling cubs just one more time,
Aah, aah, I hear them crying, oh poor things.
Creon, you good man, you pitied me!

Creon
I did, and brought them here for your delight.

Oedipus
God bless you, Creon, and shed your path with joy.
Come, children, come into your father's arms.
Poor little birds, you'll have to learn to fly
Without your father's branches in which to hide.
Poor darling ones, and when you're fully grown
What man will marry you and risk his seed
Falling into such a contaminated stream
Flowing with a murderer's tainted blood.
You face an empty destiny, poor birds,
To wander childless o'er a hostile earth.
Creon, I beg once more your generous soul,
Please be a father to them, my good friend.
You are their uncle, Jocasta's brother, their blood,
Open your heart to them and give them warmth.
Farewell my ones, you'll be always in my heart.

Creon
Enough farewells, now, Oedipus, go inside.
I'll see that they are treated well,
For my own sister's sake I could do no less.

Oedipus
Now send me off. Announce it strongly now!

Creon
    That I'll do but first release your children.

Oedipus
    I will. It's just so hard to let them go.
    I can't do it, Creon, pull them away!

Creon
    Stop it, Oedipus, stop being master now!

    Oedipus is led away.

Creon
    Citizens of our ancestral Thebes,
    I banish for all time and ever more
    The once almighty Oedipus our King,
    In accordance with the city's holy laws
    We now have purged this 'unsolved' crime
    That like some bloated and unburied corpse
    Sent plumes of stench to the gods up high.
    Now we have cleansed our house!

    Blackout.